RULES *of* THUMB

A GUIDE FOR WRITERS

First Canadian Edition

JAY SILVERMAN
Nassau Community College

ELAINE HUGHES
Nassau Community College

DIANA ROBERTS WIENBROER
Nassau Community College

COLLEEN MARLIN
Centennial College

McGraw-Hill Ryerson Limited

Toronto New York Auckland Bogotá C
Lisbon London Madrid Mexico Milan N
San Juan Singapore Sydney Tokyo

RULES OF THUMB: A GUIDE FOR WRITERS
First Canadian Edition

ISBN: 0-07-552629-8

1 2 3 4 5 6 7 8 9 10   W   5 4 3 2 1 0 9 8 7 6

Printed and bound in Canada

Care has been taken to trace ownership of copyright material contained in this text. The publisher will gladly take any information that will enable them to rectify any reference or credit in subsequent editions.

Sponsoring Editor: Dave Ward
Supervising Editor: Margaret Henderson
Production Editor: Matthew Kudelka
Developmental Editor: Laurie Graham
Production Co-ordinator: Nicla Dattolico
Text and Cover Design: Dianna Little
Typesetter: McGraphics
Printer: Webcom

Canadian Cataloguing in Publication Data

Main entry under title:

Rules of thumb

1st Canadian ed.
Includes index.
ISBN 0-07-552629-8

1. English language – Rhetoric.   2. English language – Grammar.
I. Silverman, Jay, 1947–   .

PE1408.R85   1996   808'.042   C95–933243-X

To those who want or need to write well

C O N T E N T S

HOW TO USE *RULES OF THUMB*

Grammar is a piano I play by ear, since I seem to have been out of school the year the rules were mentioned. All I know about grammar is its infinite power. To shift the structure of a sentence alters the meaning of that sentence, as definitely and inflexibly as the position of a camera alters the meaning of the object photographed.

Joan Didion, "Why I Write" (in Klaus 174)

Many of us write by ear, in much the same way that some musicians play by ear. But there are times when knowing the reasons why language or music works as it does can improve our writing or playing.

This book is for those of you who didn't quite "get" grammar when it was first taught to you at school, who have forgotten some of the rules, or who, like Didion, think you must have been away that year. This book is for you if you hate the thought of writing, or have to write, or love to write. *Rules of Thumb* is a quick reference guide that suggests how best to approach the challenge of writing, and reduces each potential writing problem to a few practical points. You can use it easily, at work, at home, or at school, and grow to feel more confident in your writing.

Rules of Thumb is best taken in small doses, as needed. It's not designed to be read in sequence or committed to memory; instead, it's a resource to flip open here or there to answer queries or challenges as they occur.

- Part One, "Preparing to Write Well: Developing Effectiveness as a Writer," suggests ways to prepare yourself for writing and ways to grow as a writer.

- Part Two, "The Process of Writing/Determining Content," will help you with both content and style—if you're stuck, if you need to make a paper longer, or if you have trouble with introductions and conclusions.

- Part Three, "Meeting Specific Requirements: Suggestions on Producing a Well-executed Document," offers help with formats and with writing under time pressure, as well as with writing research papers and essays on literature.

- Part Four, "Correctness," covers the most common mistakes writers make.

- Part Five, "Other Things That Are Good to Know," looks at an editor's proofreading symbols, at the most common errors and how to avoid them, and at how a piece of writing is evaluated. It also offers writing samples and provides space for personal lists to help you improve your writing.

Before beginning to read this book, explore the various parts at random. Get a sense of what sections may prove most useful to you.

Rules of Thumb shares ideas about all the stages of writing: generating ideas, organizing, proofreading, revising, and correcting.

Rules of Thumb doesn't attempt to delve into every little detail of grammar and usage, but it does cover the most common problems seen by employers and professors over the past decades.

Rules of Thumb aims to put explanations of these problems and their solutions into layperson's terms, so that the rules of grammar can be more easily understood and followed.

This reference book is meant to be a fast, uncomplicated, and accessible guide. Hopefully *Rules of Thumb* can quickly and comfortably help you build and measure the effectiveness of any piece of your writing.

ACKNOWLEDGEMENTS

For their careful reading and questioning of various drafts of *Rules of Thumb*, and for their continued enthusiasm, I wish to thank Dave Ward and Laurie Graham of McGraw-Hill Ryerson. I also appreciate Matthew Kudelka's expert editing; his work ensured the quality of the book.

I also appreciate the thoughtful comments of Dilys Denning, Lambton College; Chris Gellatly, Centennial College; Carol

Harder, Okanagan University College; and Mary Beth Knechtel, Vancouver Community College.

I am grateful for the inspiration extended by my colleagues in the English Department at Centennial College and offer special gratitude to two wise and generous women, Dorothy Kelleher and Georgia Watterson, for their insights, encouragement, and support.

I thank Eva and Nick Still for helping me see how important it is to be clearly heard and understood.

This book recognizes that all those who are students of life could occasionally use some guidance in saying what is in them to say.

Colleen Marlin

PART ONE

PREPARING TO WRITE WELL: DEVELOPING EFFECTIVENESS AS A WRITER

- *Why Write at All?*
- *What Makes a Strong Piece of Writing?*
- *Getting Ready*
- *Getting Started*
- *Keeping a Journal*
- *Finding Your Voice*
- *Being Specific/Adding Details*
- *Trimming Wordiness*
- *Varying Your Sentences*
- *Recognizing Clichés*
- *Eliminating Biased Language*
- *A Word of Advice*

Writing is easy; all you do is sit staring at a blank sheet of paper until the drops of blood form on your forehead.
Gene Fowler (in Winokur 8)

WHY WRITE AT ALL?

No one who has faced the blank page on an uninspired day has ever said that writing is easy. In fact, sometimes the experience is painful enough to have writers wondering why they bother to even try to commit ideas to paper.

We have many and varied reasons for writing. In all likelihood, anything we write is intended to ask for something, communicate something, persuade someone about something, or entertain someone.

In more specific terms, your job may require you to write a letter of complaint or inquiry, a memo, or a report. Your teacher may tell you to write a summary, analysis, or essay. At home, you may need to write to a utility company or provide your tenants, children, or partner with "how-to" instructions on how to set the VCR, or turn off the water, or similar.

There are times when we *must* communicate in writing so that things are said well once, so that others can access our words, so that our words are available for future reference, so that they can be utilized or evaluated.

There are also times when writing down our thoughts helps us clarify them. Sometimes we write because others expect it, need it, or demand it. Other times we write because of our own need to know what is going on inside.

I write entirely to find out what I'm thinking, what I'm looking at, what I see and what it means. What I want and what I fear.
                    Joan Didion, "Why I Write" (in Klaus 173)

WHAT MAKES A STRONG PIECE OF WRITING?

Every fine story must leave in the mind of the sensitive reader an intangible residuum of pleasure, a cadence, a quality of voice that is exclusively the writer's own, individual, unique.
Willa Cather (in Winokur 134)

If we think about why people choose to stop and listen, we're better able to understand how to motivate our readers to stop and read our work. Admittedly, good writing is a matter of taste, and what most pleases one reader won't necessarily please the next. But a casual poll will reveal the elements of strong writing to which readers respond positively.

- Something pulls the reader in; there is a point to reading the piece of writing.
- It is set out on the page so as to be easy to read.
- The writer's intention is clear, to both writer and reader.
- The meaning is clear.
- The use of language is appropriate, distinctive, specific, engaging, and correct.
- There is an innate logic to the piece, a natural development to the sequence in which information unfolds.
- The piece is truthful, authentic, and accurate.
- Something of the writer's personality, voice, and unique take on the world is visible in the writing.
- Examples are provided to support and prove what's being said.
- The reader feels like reading on; somehow the information holds significance and meaning for the reader.

- There is a payoff, a reward, for having read the piece, whether it's information gained, a concept understood, an attitude shifted, or a surprise enjoyed.

The secret of good writing is to say an old thing a new way or to say a new thing an old way.
                              Richard Harding Davis (in Winokur 133)

Many writers speak of their need to find a distinctive way of seeing the world, and to describe the world with passion, conviction, and honesty.

One prerequisite for strong writing is the urge—or at least the willingness—to share a particular piece of knowledge, a particular point of view, with others. Another is the willingness to revise one's writing. Good writers do what they must to rework a piece of writing to make it effective, meaningful, memorable, and correct.

GETTING READY

Part of being ready to write well involves leaving aside the negative self-perception that you're not a writer. Too often the labels you have given yourself, or that others have given you, block you from saying what there is in you to say.

Part of becoming a writer has to do with deciding you want to improve your skills, and being willing to experiment with just what that process could look like.

The fact that this book is in your hands suggests a certain amount of readiness. You have appreciated the benefit of having a reference to guide you through the writing process. Just as it isn't necessary to memorize every phone number you'll ever need, since you have a phone book in your possession, it isn't necessary for you to memorize every grammar or punctuation rule, or every stage in the writing process.

You may choose to have other reference books in your writing space: a good dictionary, a thesaurus, inspirational writing samples, and so on. There are other things you can do to ready your space. Try to put out of sight the sorts of things that will pull your mind away. Some people tolerate visual clutter better than others. Know yourself well enough to hide that which is too distracting.

Have sufficient space cleared for writing, whether at a desk or at the computer. Experiment with how best to situate your lamp, chair, table, and so on. Anticipate what you will need *before* you sit down; jumping up for books, paper, pen, coffee, or phone calls can pull your thoughts away and make it difficult to resume.

For some, a neutral space (i.e., away from home, work, or school) is better. Many great writers have worked in coffee shops, libraries, parks, and galleries, on buses or boats, and in other assorted places. Know yourself well enough to know where it's best for you to write.

Prepare not only your space but your schedule. Sometimes writing isn't entirely satisfying because you haven't carved out enough time for it. Name the time and the place to write. Commit to it.

Also prepare your mind. Read everything you can in advance of writing. Daydream on a variety of subjects. Be watching what works for you when you are reading others' work. Think about what is uniquely you—a special gift, talent, or personality trait— that you can bring to a piece of writing.

GETTING STARTED

Any piece of good writing involves naming a purpose, knowing the intended audience, and having something important to say. It all begins with an idea.

Watch your own life, to see how you come up with your best ideas. It may be while you are showering, cutting the lawn, on a long and boring car trip, or on the bus. It may be while you are falling asleep, or right after you wake up, or while you are listening to others or reading a good book. If you can spot and name those times when you feel most creative, you will be better prepared for the challenge of writing.

Part of getting started is to be both curious and observant. Start to really *see* and *think about* what is going on around you, and take note of what has you wondering and asking questions. Keep track of your ideas as they occur to you, and daydream about what you might choose to do with these ideas in the future.

KEEPING A JOURNAL

The aspiring writer gets into the habit of having paper and pen always at arm's reach. You may think you'll remember your great ideas, but as thoughts and life's demands crowd your mind, that essential, brilliant nugget may leave as quickly as it came. You may remember your dreams clearly upon waking but not later in the day. It is frustrating to have a good idea disappear. Write it down as it comes.

Keeping a journal helps you keep track of the good ideas and is one of the best ways to grow as a writer. A journal helps you put your thoughts and feelings into words, overcome writer's block, and develop a style. You will also discover things you didn't know—about yourself and about many topics. Some of your journal writing can later be developed into complete essays or stories.

Make your journal a record of your inward journey. Don't make it merely a daytimer or a diary. Set down your memories, your feelings, your observations, your hopes, your musings. A journal is your opportunity to try your hand at different types of writing, so aim for variety in your entries.

Some Guidelines for Keeping a Journal

- Don't wait until you have something you've been meaning to write about. Instead, write about anything that occurs to you. Aim to write two pages a day.

- Put each entry on the front of a new page, with the day and date at the top.

- Use a notebook you really like. Write in ink, using a pen you like.

- Leave wide margins so that you can go back and add related material or editorial comments.

- While you write, don't worry about correctness. Write as spontaneously and as honestly as you can, and let your thoughts and words flow freely. Remember, this journal is for *you* and will be a source of delight and inspiration in years to come. It is a record of what would otherwise be forgotten, as well as a way to develop your writing skill.

- At some point, return to what you've written and proofread it. Be certain you've said what you meant to say.

- Choose one direction to travel in each day and see where it leads you. If you have no topic, write whatever comes into your head or choose one of the suggestions from the list below.

Some Suggestions for Journal Entries

1. Blow off steam. Write about those things that make you really angry.

2. Describe someone you love.

3. Tell your favourite story about yourself when you were little.

4. State a controversial opinion that you have and then defend your position.

5. Respond to a movie, a TV program, a book, an article, a concert, a song.

6. Write a letter to someone and say what you can't say face to face.

7. Describe in full detail a place you know and love.

8. Remember on paper your very first boyfriend or girlfriend.

9. Make a list of all the things you want to do.

10. Immortalize one of your enemies in writing.

11. Relate, using present tense, a memorable dream you've had.

12. Sit in front of a drawing or painting and write down the feelings and images it evokes in you.

13. Describe yourself in a crowd.

14. Analyze the personal trait that gets you in trouble the most.

15. Relate an incident in which you were proud (or ashamed) of yourself.

16. Describe your dream house.

17. Capture on paper some object—such as a toy or piece of clothing—that you loved as a child.

18. Go all the way back: try to remember your very first experience in the world and describe how it looked to you then.

19. Make a list of your accomplishments.

20. Write down a family story. Include when and where you heard it.

21. Describe what you would take with you if you were to be away on a sailboat for a year.

22. Re-experience your favourite meal, food, or recipe on paper.

23. Set down a "here-and-now" scene: record sensory details right at the moment you're experiencing them.

24. Go to a public place and observe people. Write down your observations.

25. Put down four character names. Write a paragraph in which your four imaginary characters cross paths.

26. Relate your most pressing problem.

27. Describe your favourite article of clothing and tell why it means so much to you.

28. Describe an antique that has held meaning for you.

29. Analyze your relationship to food.

30. Write a persuasive appeal for a friend or family member to loan you his or her car for a long weekend.

31. Write about an uncle or an aunt.

32. Take an abstract idea such as delight, grief, or pride, and write down very specifically what the idea means to you.

33. Explain exactly how to do some activity you know well. Use sketches if you need to illustrate or clarify your point.

34. Write about yourself as a writer.

35. Explore several possible solutions to one of your current problems.

36. Trace the history of your (or another person's) various hairstyles.

37. Take one item from today's newspaper and write down your thoughts about it.

38. Commit yourself, in writing, to doing something you've always wanted to do but never have.

39. Explain how you feel about crying ... laughing ... fighting ... singing ...

40. Open the dictionary at random and point blindly to a word. Incorporate that word into a piece of writing.

41. Open an atlas. Select a destination at random and create an imaginary scenario for yourself in that new land.

42. Write a definition of love.

43. Explain why a certain piece of music is your favourite.

44. Listen to a piece of music. Describe the images that come to mind.

45. Describe the smell of kindergarten, a place you love, a place you hate.

46. Define a bad day.

47. Describe the perfect day.

48. Write the opening for an essay, article, or story about hair-dressers.

49. Describe the worst holiday of your life.

50. Begin a piece of writing with the words "I want ..."

51. Write lines of dialogue for two people in the same room who aren't listening to each other.

52. Give thanks for something precious. Or to someone special to you.

FINDING YOUR VOICE

Some of our past experiences at school may have negatively affected our present writing style. Often we write the way we think we're supposed to write, with big words and fancy sentences. The writing comes out awkward and impersonal and removed somehow from our real thoughts and feelings. In actual fact, good writing has the feel of a real person talking.

To find your own voice as a writer, keep these questions in mind when you write.

- Do I care about what I'm writing?

- Do I understand what I am saying? Will the reader?

- Am I saying this in plain English?

- Are these words I normally use?

- Am I saying what I know is true, not what I think others want to hear?

A great technique for developing your own voice is to read your work aloud. If you do it regularly, you'll begin to notice when other voices are intruding or when you are using roundabout phrases. In time, your sentences will gain rhythm and force. Reading aloud helps you remember that when you write, you are telling something to somebody. In this light, another good technique is to visualize a particular person and pretend you are writing directly to that person.

Good writing is *honest*. Honest writing requires you to break through your fears of what other people may think of you and to tell what you know to be true. Readers appreciate the truth when it is shared with simplicity by a writer who has given the topic careful thought and decided what is important.

BEING SPECIFIC/ADDING DETAILS

The man who writes about himself and his own time is the only man who writes about all people and about all time.
                    George Bernard Shaw (in Winokur 154)

Don't write about Man, write about a man.
                    E.B. White (in Winokur 15)

Strong writing moves either from the general to the specific or from the specific to the general. Whatever the guiding structure, it is the details, the colourful moments and examples, that give life to your ideas.

If a friend sees a film and says merely, "It's good," we feel frustrated until we know the specific reasons why it was good. We crave the details, for they help us sense what the writer has seen.

Adding Information

If someone asks for "more details," you probably have made a generalization with insufficient support. You need to slow down—to take *one* idea at a time and tell what it is based upon. You cannot assume that the reader agrees with you or knows what you're talking about. You have to say where you got your idea. This comes down to adding some of the following to support your point.

- examples
- facts
- logical reasoning
- explanation of abstract words
- real-life anecdotes

Ideas are abstract and hard to picture. To be remembered, they must be embodied in vivid and concrete language—in pictures, in facts, in real things that happened.

For example, here are three abstract statements.

> Gloria means what she says.
> The scene in the film was romantic.
> The paramecium displayed peculiar behaviour.

Now here they are made more concrete.

> Gloria means what she says. She says she hates television, and she backs it up by refusing to date any man who watches TV.
> The soft focus of the camera and the violin music in the background heightened the romance of the scene.
> Under the microscope, the paramecium displayed peculiar behaviour. It doubled in size and turned purple.

Adding Sensory Details

The best writing appeals to our five senses. Your job as a writer is to put down words that will cause the reader to see, hear, smell, taste, or feel exactly what you experienced.

You can sharpen your senses with "here and now" exercises. Observe and write exactly what you see, feel, smell, taste, and hear moment by moment. Expand your descriptions until they become very specific.

> I see a loose wire.
> I see that the wire to the right speaker isn't plugged into the amplifier.

Also, make a point of describing the world through a sense other than the one on which you usually depend.

> I feel the sun.
> I feel the sun hot on my back.

> I smell food cooking.
> I smell the aroma of garlic drifting over from the Spanish restaurant.

I don't like the taste of these potato chips.
The salt from these potato chips puckers my tongue.

I hear a noise.
I hear squeaky rubber soles coming down the hall.

This exercise will help you build the habit of including careful observation in your writing.

TRIMMING WORDINESS

Just as listeners or readers feel frustrated if you don't provide the information they want, some speakers and writers go too far in sharing every minute detail. Perhaps you have a friend who spends almost as long summarizing a film as it would have taken you to watch it. Think also about the times someone has given you directions. If the one instructing you puts in too many unnecessary steps or details, you can become overwhelmed, confused, or bored.

Reflect on which speakers and writers you admire. Chances are these communicators bring the information to life for you, without any superficial clutter yet without sacrificing meaning.

Too often we think that people are impressed by a writer who uses big words and long sentences. People are more impressed by a writer who is direct and *clear*.

There is an old but useful adage: Keep it simple.

Cut Empty Words

Some words sound good but carry no clear meaning. Omitting them will often make the sentence sharper. The following words are often merely space occupiers. Many sentences would be stronger without them.

experience	proceeded to
situation	the fact that
is a man who	really
in today's society	thing
and stuff like that	something
really	awfully

In the following examples the first version is wordy, the second version is trim.

The fire was a terrifying situation and a depressing experience
for all of us.
The fire terrified and depressed all of us.

Carmen is a person who has a tempestuous personality.
Carmen is tempestuous.

The reason she quit was because of the fact that she was sick.
She quit because of illness.

Anger is something we all feel.
We all feel anger.

Get Rid of Passive or Being Verbs

Being verbs like *is* and *are* sap the energy of your writing. They
dilute your sentences. Often you can replace *being* verbs with
forceful, colourful, active verbs.

Look out for *am, is, are, was, were, be, being, been.*

Especially watch out for *there is, there are, there were, it is, it was.*

Go through your writing and circle all of these passive, limp
verbs. Replace them with dynamic, energetic verbs. Doing so
produces a dramatic difference in any writing. Rephrasing or
combining sentences can greatly improve your work. Look for
the driving force behind the action, then choose as active a word
as possible to describe that action.

There are three people who influenced by career.
Three people influenced my career.

Michael was living in the past.
Michael lived in the past.

It is sad to see how depressed Mary is.
Mary's depression makes me sad.

His walk was unsteady.
He wobbled when he walked.

The woman is beautiful. Her hair is black and curly. Her eyes are green.
The woman's black, curly hair sets off her mysterious green eyes.

Save *being* verbs for times when you actually mean state of being.

She was born on Bastille Day.
I think; therefore, I am.
I am bushed.

Avoid Redundancy

He married his wife twelve years ago.
He married twelve years ago.

Be Direct

Tell what something *is*, rather than what it *isn't*.

Ron does not keep his apartment very neat.
Ron's apartment is a mess.

Replace Fancy or Technical Words

You can replace *abode* with *house* and *coronary thrombosis* with
heart attack and bring your paper down to earth. Some subjects
may require technical language, but in general, strive to use
everyday words.

Don't worry that your writing will be too short. For length, add
examples and further thoughts. Look at the topic from a different
point of view. Add meaningful points, not just empty words.

VARYING YOUR SENTENCES

Effective writing has energy. Part of that energy comes from choosing words carefully and then placing them to best effect. Appreciate that the same idea can be put in many different ways, and that every sentence has movable parts. To get more music or drama into your style, try reading your writing aloud. When you come across choppy or monotonous sentences, use some of the techniques described below.

Write an Important Sentence Several Ways

You can turn a sentence that troubles you into a sentence that pleases you. Instead of fiddling with a word here and a word there, try writing five completely different sentences, each with the same idea. One could be long, one short, one a generalization, one a picture, and so forth. You'll often find that your first version isn't your best. Play with several possibilities until you come up with the one you want. This technique works especially well for introductions and conclusions.

Use Short Sentences Often

For the same reason a yell in the midst of silence catches attention, short sentences can be powerful when placed close to long ones. Short sentences are a basic ingredient of good prose.

- They stand out visually from the surrounding text and thus command attention.
- They simplify ideas.
- They dramatize ideas.
- They create suspense.
- They add rhythm.

If you're getting tangled in too many words, a few short sentences will often get you through. Remember, however, that you must use a period between sentences, even when they're very short.

It was a rainy Monday. I was sitting at my desk. I heard a knock at the door. I waited. The doorknob turned.

Lengthen Choppy Sentences

Using *only* short sentences can make your writing monotonous. Contrast and variety are important in effective writing. Sometimes a parent, instead of calling a child's usual nickname, will haul out the entire name—first, middle, and last name parts—to get attention. Contrast and variety are important in effective speaking and conversation, and the same is true in writing. If you want to lengthen a sentence, add concrete information.

Nick!
Nicholas Charles Still, you little monkey, get over here!

Billy was popular with the girls.
Billy, with his slick hair and even slicker talk, was popular with the eighth-grade girls in the back of the school bus.

The book was boring.
The author's long descriptions of rooms in which nothing and no one ever moved made the book boring.

Combine Choppy Sentences

One option is to merge two short sentences by putting a semicolon between them.

They wanted black; I wanted pink.

Or use a comma followed by one of these connectors—

but   and   for   or   so   yet   nor

They wanted black, but I wanted pink.

Or you could use a semicolon followed by a transition word and a comma. Here are the most common transition words.

however	for	example
therefore	furthermore	nevertheless
instead	in other words	meanwhile
on the other hand	besides	

> They wanted black; on the other hand, I wanted pink.
> They wanted black; however, I wanted pink.

A second option is to highlight the major point. Often sentences contain two or more facts. You can show the relationship between these facts so that the most important one stands out. One idea becomes the dominant idea; the other becomes *subordinate*, or secondary, to the primary idea. In the following examples, two ideas are given equal weight.

> I docked my sailboat, and the hurricane hit.
> I love Earl. He barks at the slightest sound.
> Brad lost a contact lens. He had one blue eye and one brown eye.

Here are the same ideas with one point emphasized.

> Just as I docked my sailboat, the hurricane hit.
> I love Earl even though he barks at the slightest sound.
> Because Brad lost a contact lens, he had one blue eye and one brown eye.

Notice that the halves of these sentences can be reversed. *Because* can start either the first or the second half of a sentence. Other words that work the same way are *if, although, when, while,* and *whereas*:

> Although she didn't study, she aced the exam.
> She aced the exam although she didn't study.

> If it rains Saturday, we'll have a picnic at home.
> We'll have the picnic at home if it rains Saturday.

Usually the sentence gains strength when the most interesting point comes last.

A third option is to highlight one idea by *inserting* the gist of one sentence inside another.

Sheila makes a fine living as a model. She is thin. She has high cheekbones.
Sheila, who is thin and has high cheekbones, makes a fine living as a model.

The problem with most choppy sentences is that one after another starts with the subject—in this case, *Sheila* or *she*. Sometimes you can use *who* (for people) or *which* (for things) to start an insertion. Sometimes you can reduce the insertion to a word or two.

I interviewed Nell Partin, who is the mayor.
I interviewed Nell Partin, the mayor.

Give Your Sentences a Strong Ending

The beginning is worth sixty cents, and what's in the middle is worth forty cents, but the end is worth a dollar.

I walked into the room, looked around at all the flowers my friends had sent, took a deep breath, and collapsed into a chair in tears.

When the nights grow cool and foggy and the full moon rises after the day's harvest, Madeline, so the story goes, roams the hills in search of revenge.

What Louie received, after all the plea-bargaining and haggling and postponements and hearings, was a ten-year sentence.

To stress the most important parts of your sentence, tuck in interrupters or insertions. Put transitions or minor information in the middle of your sentence.

He argues, as you probably know, even with statues.
From my point of view, however, that's a mistake.
The interior decoration, designed by his cousin, looked gaudy.

Remember to put commas on both sides of the insertion.

Use Parallel Structure

Parallel structure—repeating certain words for clarity and emphasis—makes for strong sentences. The elements in a sentence should feel as if they belong together. Strive for symmetry in your phrasing. It makes your sentences both more meaningful and more rhythmic. Parallel structure is especially important when you are writing the traditional three-point thesis.

No political party, whether of the left, the centre, or the right, has an inherent right to govern.

Whether you have a passion for sailing, hiking, or skiing, you'll find something adventurous to do, only half an hour from downtown Vancouver.

To be honest is not necessarily to be brutal.

Famous quotations are often based on parallel structure.

I came, I saw, I conquered. — Julius Caesar

To believe your own thought, to believe that what is true for you in your private heart is true for all men—that is genius. — Emerson

RECOGNIZING CLICHÉS

Clichés come into being because someone, sometime, had a good idea and expressed it well. When we get lazy in our speech or writing, we tend to fall back on other people's words. A cliché is a *predictable* word, phrase, or statement. If it sounds very familiar, if it comes very easily, it's probably a cliché. Clichés are comfortable—often so old that they are in our bones—and they are usually true.

But because clichés are predictable, the reader loses concentration when reading them. In going over your writing, try to replace clichés with fresher, sharper descriptions. Make your descriptions your own. Remember, good writing happens when you say in a unique way what is in you to say. When you succeed in that, others will be tempted to borrow from *you*.

Recognize Clichés

The best way to spot clichés is to make a list of all the ones you hear. Clichés fall into groups.

Comparisons—

cold as ice	slept like a log
drunk as a skunk	fought like a tiger
hot as ...	smooth as silk

Pairs—

hot and heavy	by leaps and bounds
apples and oranges	wining and dining

Images—

raining cats and dogs
up the creek without a paddle
lives in a pigsty
between a rock and a hard place

Sayings—

There are other fish in the sea.
Read my lips ...
No use crying over spilt milk.
Welcome to the club.

Lines—

What's a nice girl like you doing in a place like this?
Haven't I met you somewhere before?
We've got to stop meeting like this.
Come here often?

Phrases—

madly in love	ripe old age
easier said than done	with bated breath

"In" words—

fantastic	wow	no way	groovy
awesome	like	for sure	totally
wonderful	really	radical	Not!

This year's new expression is next year's cliché. If the phrase is really out of style, readers will laugh when they read it.

We use clichés when we want to play it safe (for example, when making conversation or writing for an unfamiliar audience) or when we haven't managed to find a better, more individual way to say something. We tend to resort to clichés in potentially uncomfortable situations such as first dates, funerals, beginnings of parties, and when writing.

Eliminate Clichés

- Often you can simply omit the cliché—you don't need it. The essay is better without it.

- At other times, replace the cliché by saying what you mean. Give the details. Make your writing fresh, new, unique, representative of your individual way of expressing yourself.

- Look out for clichés in your conclusion, where they tend to gather. By the conclusion, sometimes you've run out of the energy to express yourself well.

- Make up your own comparisons and descriptions. Have fun writing creatively, from your own sensations and point of view.

To gain experience, list several of the clichés most familiar to you. Experiment with language to catch the same meaning with different words and phrasing. See how many different ways there are of saying a similar thing.

ELIMINATING BIASED LANGUAGE

No doubt there have been times when you heard or read something that offended you. People made comments you didn't appreciate or cracked jokes you didn't find funny. Or perhaps they said things that in your mind are false and discriminatory.

When writing, show your sensitivity to your audience in your choice of words. Avoid using biased language, which includes all expressions that demean or exclude people. To avoid offending your readers, examine both the words you use and their underlying assumptions.

Offensive Word Choices

Some wording is prejudiced or impolite or outdated.

- Eliminate name-calling, slurs, and derogatory nicknames. Instead, refer to groups by the names they use for themselves. For example, use *women* (not *chicks*), *Jamaican Canadians* or *blacks* (not *coloured people*), and *native people* (not *Indians*).

- Replace words using *man* or *ess* with nonsexist terms. For example, use *flight attendant* (not *stewardess*), *mechanic* (not *repairman*), *chairperson* (not chairman), and *humanity* (not *mankind*).

False Assumptions

Some statements are based on hidden biases. Look hard at references to any group—even one you belong to. Acknowledge that every member of a group does not believe or look or behave exactly like every other member.

- Check for stereotypes about innate abilities or flaws in members of a group. For example, all women are not maternal, and all lawyers are not unscrupulous. Many clichés—absent-minded professor, dumb jock, and so on—are based on stereotypes.

- Do not imply that certain jobs are filled by certain groups or by one sex. All nurses aren't women, all mechanics aren't men, and all milk store owners aren't immigrants. Don't write *female judge* as you would be saying that all judges are male unless named. For the same reason, don't write *male nurse*.

- In a pair or list, watch for inconsistency.

Not—

man and wife

Instead, use—

man and woman   or   husband and wife

Not—

two Conservatives, a Liberal, a woman, and a black

This list assumes that everyone is a white man unless otherwise specified. Instead, use—

two Conservatives and a Liberal

Faulty Pronouns

Check pronouns for bias.

Each Supreme Court justice should have *his* clerk make copies of the decision.

One option for revision is to use *his or her*.

Each Supreme Court justice should have *his or her* clerk make copies of the decision.

A more graceful solution is to use the plural throughout.

The Supreme Court justices should have *their* clerks make copies of the decision.

Sometimes you can eliminate the pronoun.

A senior citizen can get *his* ticket at half-price.

That is weak. Instead, use—

A senior citizen can get a ticket at half-price.

You can find more help with pronoun choice in the section "Consistent Pronouns."

A WORD OF ADVICE

Analyze the Work of Good Writers

Again, one of the best ways to develop your own writing is to take a close look at some of your favourite authors. A good exercise is to pick out a sentence or a paragraph that you particularly like. Read it aloud once or twice; then copy it over several times to get the feel of the language. Now study it closely and try to write a piece of your own, incorporating those elements and techniques you most admire. Use the sentence or paragraph as a model, but think up your own ideas and words. This exercise can rapidly expand your power to vary your sentences.

PART TWO

THE PROCESS OF WRITING/ DETERMINING CONTENT

- *"Just Do It"*
- *Scattergrams, Umbrellas, and Spills*
- *What to Do When You're Stuck*
- *Time Wasters: What Not to Do*
- *The Importance of Research*
- *Finding Your Thesis*
- *Finding an Organization for Your Essay*
- *Intros, Middles, and Conclusions*
- *Introductions*
- *Middles*
- *Conclusions*
- *How to Work on a Second Draft*
- *How to Make a Paper Longer (or Shorter)*
- *Transitions*
- *Proofreading Tips*

"JUST DO IT"

You have spent some time thinking about what makes good writing. You've decided you're ready to write. You've prepared your space. You know what's required of you. You've named your intention. You know your audience. Now what?

Not being entirely sure what it is you have to say can hold you back from sitting down to write. Many people procrastinate because of uncertainty about what they should write.

The best advice is this: sit down and begin. As the Nike slogan suggests, "Just do it." Remember, it is through the process of writing that you will discover what it is that's begging to be said. You won't know until you begin.

SCATTERGRAMS, UMBRELLAS, AND SPILLS

Write freely and as rapidly as possible and throw the whole thing on paper. Never correct or rewrite until the whole thing is down. Rewrite in process is usually found to be an excuse for not going on.

John Steinbeck (in Winokur 14)

Too often, we prevent ourselves from writing by being overly self-critical too early in the process. Too often, we are our own worst critics; our fear of not doing well prevents us from taking the plunge. You must warm up to the process, stick your toe in the water, puddle and wade for a bit. Soon you will feel ready to dive in.

Part of the warm-up is to play around with possible ideas. Select a general topic. Now brainstorm with yourself. Take a piece of paper and jot down ideas as they come to you, without censoring or criticizing. Fill the page with random, rambling thoughts, catching them as they flutter in and before they can flutter out again. From this page of scribbles, this scattergram, you'll get closer to feeling ready to write. Your brain will now be in drive, not neutral or park. As you look over the page, associations will come; good ideas will jump out at you.

If you were to write a scattergram about teenage pregnancy, your scattergram might look something like this.

end of education	money troubles
people making judgments	abortion
social assistance	parental pressure
growing up too fast	birth control
religion	where to live
clothes don't fit	changes to body
friends leave you behind	responsibility
adoption	benefits
being close in age to child	children having children

support   young fathers
what you need   names
public attitude   phases in pregnancy
necessary supplies   advantages/disadvantages
what if mother-to-be doesn't
   want baby but father-to-be does
healthy young mother,
   healthy baby

The list of possibilities goes on and on. The process of seeing the many directions you could travel in, and then selecting which thread you want to follow, is important to building a strong piece of writing.

Once some options are made visible, ask yourself these questions.

• Which concept is the most predictable? Which have already been adequately examined? You can eliminate these options, unless you see a way to make the old, traditional, and expected look new, distinctive, and yours.

• Which items seem related? Which can be placed under the same umbrella?

• Which item holds the most energy for you? Which direction interests you the most?

• Which items on your list can you find out more about? Will you be able to back up your point of view?

Once you have narrowed your choices slightly, spill related thoughts on paper. Let the words fall out of you, without your judging them. Play with your ideas. See where your thoughts take you.

WHAT TO DO WHEN YOU'RE STUCK

Sometimes the ideas don't seem to be there, or you have only two ideas, or your thoughts are disconnected and jumbled. Sometimes it's hard to know where to begin or what shape your writing should take. Sometimes you just can't decide what it is you want to say.

Here are some techniques used by professional writers. Try several. Some are better for particular writing tasks. For instance, lists and outlines work when you don't have much time (in an essay exam) or when you have many points to include. "Freewriting" works well when your topic is subtle, when you want to write with depth.

Freewriting

In this method, you find your ideas by writing without a plan, quickly, without stopping. Don't worry about what to say first. Start somewhere in the middle. Just write nonstop for ten to twenty minutes. Ignore grammar, spelling, organization. Follow your thoughts as they come. Above all, don't stop! If you hit a blank place, write your last word over and over—you'll soon have a new idea. After you freewrite, write one sentence that begins, "The main point I'm making is ..."

When you've freewritten several times, read your writing and search out the strongest ideas and underline the good sentences. These can be the heart of the piece. You can make a list of them and toy with the order of your final essay.

Freewriting takes time, but it is the easiest way to begin and leads to surprising and creative results. Without it, you can be stopped by your own judgments. The hat of creator and that of editor are very different. If you edit prematurely, you'll lose the flow, the energy will fly away on you, and you'll have a tough time getting back into the rhythm of the piece. Be gentle with yourself. Create first. Criticize later.

The habit of compulsive, premature editing doesn't just make writing hard. It also makes writing dead. Your voice is damped out by all the interruptions, changes, and hesitations between the consciousness and the page. In your natural way of producing words there is a sound, a texture, a rhythm—a voice—which is the main source of power in your writing. I don't know how it works, but this voice is the force that will make a reader listen to you, the energy that drives the meaning through ...
Peter Elbow, "Freewriting" (in Bloom 72)

Lists and Outlines

Before you write any sentences, reflect on your intention and topic. Make a list of the points you might use in your essay, report, or letter, including any examples and details that come to mind. Jot them down, a word or phrase for each item. Keeping these points brief makes them easier to read and rearrange. Include any ideas you think of in one long list down the page. When you run dry, wait a little——more ideas will come.

Now start grouping the items on the list. Draw lines to connect the examples to the points they illustrate. Then make a new list with the related points grouped together. Decide which idea is most important and cross out ideas or details that do not relate to it. Arrange your points so that each will lead to the next. Be sure each section of your essay has examples or facts to strengthen your ideas.

You're ready to write. This system works best when you have a big topic with many details. Although it seems complicated, it actually saves time. Once you have your plan, the writing will go very quickly.

Working from a Core Paragraph

Write just one paragraph—at least six sentences—that tells the main ideas you have in mind. Arrange the sentences in a logical and effective sequence. Then copy each sentence from that core paragraph onto its own page and write a paragraph to back up each sentence. Now you have the rough draft of an essay.

The purpose of your paper is to convince the reader of your point. Your goal in organizing is to produce a sequence of paragraphs presenting your point one step at a time. There are many ways to reach this goal.

Some people need an outline; others write first and then reorganize when they see a pattern in their writing. Still others begin in the middle or write the different sections out of order.

No method is the "right" one. Some approaches are better for certain topics; some are better for certain people. Do not feel that you have to fit into a set way of working.

Using a Tape Recorder

If you have trouble writing as fast as you think, talk your ideas into a recorder. Play them back several times, stopping to write down the best sentences. Another method is to write down four or five sentences before you begin, each starting with the main word of your topic but otherwise different from the others. Use these sentences to get going when you run dry and to make sure you discuss different aspects of your topic.

A Relaxation Technique to Clear Your Mind

Often writing is made more difficult by the clutter in our minds. This technique may help you let go of those distracting thoughts so that new ideas can visit you: Sit up straight in a chair, put your feet flat on the floor, and place your palms on your thighs. Breathe very slowly, feeling the air spiral through your body. Focus on a spot on the floor. Feel each part of your body relax, starting with your feet. Take your time. Listen to the most distant sounds you can hear, the faintest sounds. Do this for several minutes, ears open, muscles relaxing, concentrating on your slow breathing. Then take a deep breath and begin to freewrite.

Talking to a Friend

The idea here is for your friend to help you discover and organize *your* ideas—not to tell you his or her ideas. The best person for this is not necessarily a good writer; however, he or she must be a good listener. Ask your friend just to listen and not say anything for a few minutes. As you talk, you might jot down points you make. Then ask what came across most vividly. As your friend responds, you may find yourself saying more, trying to make a point clearer. Make notes of the new points, but don't let your friend write or dictate words for you. Once you have plenty of notes, you're ready to be alone and to freewrite or outline. You can go through the same internal conversation with yourself if no friend is available, by talking through your ideas.

Making a Change

If you're having difficulties ... try the element of surprise: attack it at an hour when it isn't expecting it.
H.G. Wells (in Winokur 15)

Sometimes we try too hard. Forcing thoughts doesn't necessarily help thoughts come. Try making a change instead. Something as simple as moving your chair or taking your pad of paper out to the nearest café can free your blocked mind. It may be useful to make more rough notes, take a short walk, read for a bit, have a nap, go for a drive—anything to leave the idea for the moment. Return to it when it doesn't feel so watched or conscious. Sometimes if you labour over your writing and worry about not being able to write, you slow yourself down unnecessarily. Be kind to yourself: give yourself a break, let the idea incubate for a bit, go back to it, and give yourself a reward once you manage to take your concept further.

TIME WASTERS: WHAT NOT TO DO

Avoid Redecorating

Many people talk about their avoidance techniques. Suddenly the socks get sorted and the basement gets cleaned … we can all find so many excuses to avoid sitting down and writing. Instead of jumping into another project, lure yourself to your writing table and plan a reward for after. Once you begin, the process is not so painful. For many, sitting down to write is the hardest part of the process.

Don't Spend Hours on an Outline

You will probably revise your outline after the first draft, so don't get bogged down at the beginning. If the outline is too specific and detailed, it can feel as if you've already written the paper, and the actual writing can seem overly repetitious and monotonous. Give yourself a sense of the direction you are planning on taking, a roadmap, but leave space for surprises and shifts. Even with long papers, a topic outline (naming the idea for each paragraph without supporting details) is often a more efficient way to organize.

If you use note cards, arrange them according to the paragraph topics they support, rather than copying them onto an outline. A corkboard comes in handy so that you can pin the cards up in the anticipated sequence. You can easily rearrange the cards to see which order is most logical and pleasing.

Don't Recopy Repeatedly

Get down a complete first draft before you try to revise any of it. Write on every second or third line so that you can revise easily. Keep a sheet of note paper handy to jot down new thoughts when they occur, and place a number or star to mark the places where you plan to insert new thoughts.

Don't Use a Dictionary, Thesaurus, or Grammar Reference Book Before the Second Draft

Delay your concern for spelling and precise wording until you have the whole paper written. Then go back and make improvements. If you become an editor before you've created the whole, you can too easily lose your direction, energy, and style. Create first. Improve later.

Don't Try to Make Only One Draft

You may think you can save time by writing only one draft, but you can't get everything perfect the first time. Actually, it's faster to write something *approximately* close to the points you want to make, then go back and revise.

Don't Write with Distractions

When you write, you need to focus your brainpower and physical energy. You can be distracted by music, television, the telephone, or conversation in the background; or perhaps you are too uncomfortable or too comfortable. Distractions waste time by diffusing your energy and concentration. Prepare yourself and your space before beginning to write.

Don't Find Yourself with Nothing to Say

Writing is a painful experience when you don't have a burning desire to say something. If you are drawing a blank, chances are there is a better focus or take on the subject than the one you began with. Reconsider your way into the paper until you find yourself with lots to say.

Keeping a journal is one way to ensure that you're never at a loss for something to write about. Another way is to ask yourself questions, wonder aloud, listen, observe, read, seek answers.

THE IMPORTANCE OF RESEARCH

Research will help you find both the general idea and the specific content for any piece of writing. Research can take many shapes. You could spend an afternoon in the local library, reading books, journals, newspapers, encyclopedias, novels. You could talk to the person sitting next to you on the bus. You could eavesdrop on a conversation. You could listen to a radio program, watch a documentary. You could look at what's already been written on the same subject. You could ask yourself what *hasn't* been written.

No matter how you access information, be sure to accurately note what you heard or read in a clear and thorough way. Also, write down every available detail about the source of the information. If your research has been published, take note of the author's name, the title, the city in which it was published, the publisher, the year of publication, and the page number.

Be on the lookout for inconsistencies in the information you gather. Don't settle for one outlook on the topic—look further. Be alert for less obvious sources that could add depth or interest to your paper.

Always remember the purpose of your writing—to entertain, inform, and/or persuade. Also, that the nature of your audience must affect what you say and how you say it. Whatever your purpose, audience, or topic, ask yourself these questions: Who? What? Where? When? Why? How? Then make the effort to hunt out the answers.

FINDING YOUR THESIS

For those who are uncertain where to go in their writing, a thesis statement can save hours of confusion. A thesis statement is like a blueprint or a road map. It is one or more sentences in the introductory paragraph that tell the reader what the piece of writing is about and what direction it will take. It is what gives the essay, letter, or report its focus. Every piece of writing requires this kind of structure.

Name a Topic, and Ask General Questions About It

To find a workable thesis, start by naming the general topic. Then ask yourself some specific questions about the topic, study your answers, and choose three related points from your answers. An illustration of this process follows.

General Topic: Friends
Possible Questions:

1. What can one expect from a friendship?
2. What is the definition of a friend?
3. Why can you choose your friends but not your family?
4. Where do friends go on moving day?
5. How can you say "no" to a friend?
6. Why do some friendships last, and some just fade away?
7. What role do friendships play in one's life?
8. What do my friends have in common?
9. How do I pick my friends?

Go through your list until one question catches your attention. Seek out the question with *energy*—the one that holds particular interest for you.

List Points That Answer the Question

List some points that come to mind when you are contemplating the selected question.

Response to question #1:
What can one expect from a friendship?

sensitivity	depth of feeling
understanding	fun
sharing	honesty
surprises	support
encouragement	flexibility
strength	everything
nothing	laughter
tears	silence
dinners out	all the emotions at once
comfort	a chance to know oneself better

Reorganize Your Points

Now look for any overlap. Arrange your points in categories.

Grouping 1: sensitivity, depth of feeling, understanding, sharing, honesty, support, encouragement, strength, a chance to know oneself better, comfort

Grouping 2: fun, sharing, surprises, laughter, dinners out

Grouping 3: everything, nothing

Grouping 4: laughter, tears, silence

Look over each grouping and decide which one holds the most interest for you. Then spend some time considering what these points could open up to in an essay, article, report, or letter.

Which points seem too similar? (If they are too similar, you'll end up repeating yourself.) Which points seem too dissimilar? (If they are too different from one another, you'll have a tough time using them to support one underlying theme.)

Be selective. Limit yourself to a natural grouping of two or three, then work them into your statement of what will follow. Select points that are distinctive enough that you won't be repetitious or boring in your writing; but at the same time, be sure those points speak to the same issue and belong together in the same piece of writing.

Sample Thesis Statements

(based on Grouping 1)

> A true friendship is a relationship in which two people are honest, sensitive, and supportive enough that each has a better chance to truly know both self and friend.

From this thesis statement, a reader would expect to find the first body paragraph dealing with the importance of honesty in a friendship, the second talking about the need for sensitivity, the third about the importance of support, and the conclusion wrapping up how each component contributes to knowledge of self and friend.

(based on Grouping 2)

> My best friend is more than a little outrageous. Together, we can get into anything and everything. But one can be certain that no matter what we do together, we'll have fun.

While surprises, laughter, and dinners out aren't specifically named in the thesis, it would be quite possible for the writer to offer specific anecdotes to show the variety of possible events in a close and fun friendship.

(based on Grouping 3)

> In any friendship, one can expect everything and nothing.

When this is introduced somewhere in an opening paragraph, one can assume that the first portion of the essay will explain all the great things one wants in a friendship, and the second portion will elaborate on all those things one can't expect to find.

(based on Grouping 4)

We laugh. We cry. We sit in silence. Friendship leaves space for it all.

This thesis would remind you, as writer, to devote a paragraph to how laughter is a part of friendship, another to how tears are a part of friendship, and a third to the role of silence in friendship.

The above sample thesis statements give you a sense of the variety of directions it is possible to take your paper. An essay can be only as strong as its original thesis. Take care in its selection.

Remember again that the thesis charts the course for your journey. It lets you know where to take your writing. When the readers read your thesis, they'll know clearly what you intend to talk about. When you refer to your thesis, you'll know what to do in each paragraph of your piece of writing.

A thesis statement is the driving force behind your whole piece of writing. If you don't feel engaged with it at the stage of naming it, you haven't found the best thesis for your topic. In some cases you will have to go back and extend your scattergram to discover new points. In other cases you may just need to regroup—to spot a different connection than the one previously most visible.

Reconsidering Your Choice of Thesis

Sometimes the first thought on a thesis isn't the best. A good thesis can evolve if you spend a little time walking around the topic at hand and then take another look at it from a different angle.

Before firming up your thesis statement, ask yourself these questions.

- Is it focused? Are you examining one main point or do you have a cluttered or obscure notion of the topic at hand?

- Is it original? Are you looking at the topic in your own unique way—at the world according to *you*?

- Is it meaningful? Will a reader care to read it and be affected by it?

- Is it supportable? Is there enough information and evidence available to you to back up what you're trying to say or prove?

Thesis Creation Checklist

Use the formula below to design an interesting, workable thesis statement.

General topic:

_____

_____

_____

_____

Topic with focus narrowed slightly:

_____

_____

_____

_____

General questions to ask about this more specific topic:

1. _____

2. _____

3. _____

4. _____

5. _____

6. _____

Question that holds the most energy, interest:

_____

_____

Points that answer the question:

_____

_____

_____

_____

_____

Similar points grouped together:

_____

_____

_____

_____

Grouping that has the most energy and interest (rephrase points so that they are related but distinct):

_____

_____

_____

_____

Three points from your list of favourites (for a five-paragraph essay):
1. _____
2. _____
3. _____

Points in logical sequence, perhaps climactic (second-strongest > third-strongest > strongest) or chronological (first > second > third thing to happen):

Point to be developed in _first_ body paragraph:

_____

_____

Point to be developed in _second_ body paragraph:

_____

_____

Point to be developed in _third_ body paragraph:

_____

_____

Points rewritten in sentence form:

_____

_____

_____

_____

Review the first draft of your thesis statement. Remember **FOMS**:
— Focused
— Original
— Meaningful
— Supportable

1. Is your thesis narrowed, focused, specific?

   Yes ☐   No ☐

2. Is your thesis distinctive, fresh, original, unique to you?

   Yes ☐   No ☐

3. Is your thesis important, profound, meaningful, worth exploring, writing, reading?

   Yes ☐   No ☐

4. Will you be able to find accurate, important, and interesting information, examples, anecdotes, facts, evidence to help you support and prove your point?

   Yes ☐   No ☐

Rephrase your thesis, making it as useful, distinctive, and interesting as possible:

_____

_____

_____

_____

_____

_____

FINDING AN ORGANIZATION FOR YOUR ESSAY

Any essay is a piece of persuasive writing. You, as writer, are persuading readers to read on, to accept your thesis or underlying concept or idea, to believe you, and in many cases to change their point of view to match yours.

Advertisers make use of the AIDA formula when deciding how to organize any persuasive message.

> First, one must attract   ATTENTION
> next, create   INTEREST
> then motivate   DESIRE and
> finally, prompt   ACTION or AFFECT ATTITUDE

You can apply this formula to many types of persuasive writing.

When to Use a Formula and When to Make Up Your Own Plan

Sometimes you are given a format to follow. For instance, lab reports often start with the question to be investigated; they then describe the experiment to be tried, follow with the observations, and end with the conclusions. Other times you discover a pattern that you can repeat for similar assignments. A formula is especially useful for assignments you must do quickly. But for many topics you will need to discover the best plan by making lists of ideas and reordering them, or by writing for a while and then reworking what you've written.

How to Make Your Own Plan

Here's a method that works for many writers.

- Make a random list—written in *phrases*, not sentences—of all the ideas and facts you want to include. Don't be stingy—make a *long* list.

- Now look at your list and decide which items are your main points and which are your supporting points.

- Write a sentence or two containing the main point you are going to make. Make sure this point is stated early in your essay.

- Decide on the order of your main points. Sometimes you will want to put your points in *chronological* order—that is, in the sequence in which events occurred. Other times you will want to put them in *dramatic* order, building to the strongest point. You can start with generalizations and work your way to specifics, or vice versa.

Some topics lend themselves to particular arrangements. These arrangements are sometimes referred to as rhetorical modes. Here are a few of the modes available to you as a writer.

narration: Tell a story that really happened.

thesis: When I was five, my father came home and announced with glee that I now had a baby brother. I knew in a flash that my life as I'd known it was over. I was embarking on a new phase, that of being not the baby, but the middle child.

description: Describe a person, place, situation, or concept in detail.

thesis: There was pain in going back. Now the house stood, windows broken, choked by persistent vines, its front door off its hinges, in need of paint. I couldn't reconcile this abandoned shell with the happy home of my early childhood.

illustration and example: Make a point, and back it up with real-life examples.

thesis: Motherhood can be especially traumatic for the first year. A dramatic percentage of women suffer from postpartum depression. For many more, this period can negatively affect self-esteem and result in an identity crisis. Most women suffer from overwhelming fatigue. It's a wonder that so many women go on to have a second child.

process analysis: Give the steps for how something is done: first this, then this, then this.

thesis: When learning to drive a standard, one must understand the rules of the road, explore the relationship between the clutch, the shifting of gears, and the action of the motor, and be prepared to practise in a borrowed car.

comparison: Show similarities and differences.

thesis: In each of Margaret Atwood's novels, the leading ladies have some rather profound and complicated problems. That being said, all the characters in *The Handmaid's Tale, Cat's Eye,* and *The Robber Bride* respond in unique ways to the challenges at hand.

pro and con: Show advantages and disadvantages.

thesis: Many urbanites are having second thoughts about city life and are choosing to move to the country. They won't miss the bad air and chaos. They may miss the stimulation and variety.

classification: Show types and categories.

thesis: Mechanics scratch their heads in bewilderment and frustration over three kinds of monstrous cars: those which look and sound fine to the mechanic but not to the owner; those which suffer an illness nearly impossible to diagnose; and those which are lemons, plain and simple, on which all efforts are futile.

definition: Explain the meaning of a term or issue.

thesis: A bad day is one when you don't have enough hot water for your shower, can't get the words coming out right, get yelled at and so in turn yell at a friend, and at the end of the day, decide it would have been better if you'd just stayed in bed.

problem and solution: Spell out the dilemma, then logically build to concrete ideas on resolution.

thesis: Insomnia affects an increasing percentage of Canadians. Experts in sleeping disorders suggest watching stressors and diet, removing yourself from the bedroom when you can't sleep, and devising an assortment of relaxation exercises to help discourage insomnia.

cause and effect: Show the relationship between an action or situation and its consequence.

thesis: In times of economic hardship, we must expect an increase in crime.

appealing to reason: Find the logical facts to stimulate and persuade the reader's intellect.

thesis: We've had it easy. We have taken what we wanted from the earth, without thinking of the effects our actions could have on its future. But now we know better. If we don't demonstrate new sensitivity to the health of our earth, water, and air, none of these will be fit for future generations.

appealing to emotion: Use charismatic and emotional appeals and go straight for the heart.

thesis: Take a walk through any seniors home. You'll see old people waiting for a visitor, waiting for lunch, waiting to die. This period can be a long, lonely, and confusing one. Volunteers help make this final stage of life more comfortable and pleasurable.

critical argument/textual analysis: Analyze another's work.

thesis: Leonard Cohen, in his poems, songs, and novels, has a richness of language, a dark and desperate romanticism, and a distinctive tone of awe.

No matter what type of essay you choose to write, once you have selected your thesis, carry on with the next steps.

- Cross off points from your list that do not fit the pattern or plan you are using. Remember, you can't put in everything you know.

- Decide on your paragraphs; write a sentence for each paragraph that tells what you plan to say. This guiding sentence for each paragraph is known as the *topic sentence*.

- Now start writing. Get a rough draft finished before you reconsider your organization.

When to Adjust Your Plan

Sometimes the trick to good organization is *reorganization*. No matter whether you start with an outline, no matter what you think when you begin, your topic may well change as you write. Often you will come up with better ideas; as a result, you may change your emphasis. You must be ready to abandon parts or all of your original plan. Some minor points may now become major points. Most writers need to revise their plan *after* they finish a first draft.

In the end, make sure that you know the main point you want the reader to get and that every sentence contributes to making that point clear.

The Order of Your Points

If you have trouble getting from one main point to the next, you may need to omit one point or move your points around.

- Make a list of your points in the order you wrote them.
- Now play with the order so that each one seems well placed.
- Get rid of points that aren't related.
- Cover some points briefly as parts of other points.

Make sure that the steps of your thinking are clear, complete, and logical. Here are some sequences you might try.

Choices in How to Structure an Essay

If you decide on an organizational scheme before you begin to write, you will find it easier to find the right places for your points.

climactic: Start with the second-strongest point, have the less strong ones in the middle, and save the best and biggest and most influential point until last.

anticlimactic: Start with the strongest and go on from there.

chronological: Either start in the present and work backwards, or start in the most distant past and work forwards.

spatial: Consider the physical make-up of the thing discussed in the topic; then start with east and move west, or at the top and move down, or inside and move outside (etc.).

question/answer: Pose the question, answer it immediately, and move on to the next question.

pro/con: Name and discuss the advantages and disadvantages; argue both sides.

process of elimination: Find arguments *against* the point of view that is contrary to the one you are attempting to prove in your essay.

withheld proposal: Withhold till the end what you are trying to prove.

INTROS, MIDDLES, AND CONCLUSIONS

Any essay has three main parts to it: the opening, the middle, and the closing. How you get into your paper, and how you get out of it, are especially important. If you can get these right, often the middle will take care of itself.

After you've written your paper, pretend that you are a reader leafing through a magazine. Would you stop to read your paper? Would you lose interest at the end? You may need to rework your piece of writing so that the introduction grabs the reader's interest and the conclusion puts what you've written into meaningful, memorable perspective.

To get a strong first or last sentence, try writing a few different sentences. They can express the same basic idea, but they should be worded as differently as possible—one long, one short, one plain, one elegant. Write several, playing with thought and language until you find the best way to say what you want to say.

INTRODUCTIONS

When you're flipping through a magazine, you may pass by many articles before you decide to read one. Perhaps the title or photo or illustration attracted you first. But it is what is contained in the first paragraph that determines whether you read on.

The introduction has two primary functions: to grab and hold the attention of the reader; and to give both writer and reader a sense of the direction the piece of writing will take.

In an essay exam or under time pressure, write the introduction first to indicate the map of the paper. In a longer essay, taking time with the introduction may trigger the whole essay and tell you what you want to say. Sometimes you may get stuck writing an introduction. In that case, try writing it *after* you've written the rest of the first draft. Often you don't find your real main point until you've written several pages.

Here are a few common methods for beginning an essay.

Indicate the Parts

In academic papers and in technical or business reports, the introduction should indicate what is coming. Write a brief paragraph summing up the points you plan to make, one at a time. Then, in the middle of your paper, give each point a paragraph.

> There were three causes of the sudden population increase in 18th-century Europe. First, the newly settled colonies provided enough wealth to support more people. Second, 18th-century wars did not kill as many Europeans as did 17th-century wars. Finally, the introduction of the potato provided a cheap food source.

Sometimes you can indicate the parts of your essay more subtly.

> Lucy Maud Montgomery's tales are still widely read today. The liveliness of her dialogue, depth of her characters, and her insightful treatment of universal themes contribute to the timelessness of her stories.

W.O. Mitchell has written many novels. He is probably best known for his first, *Who Has Seen the Wind*, which follows the boy Brian as he learns about birth, death, and life.

Take a Bold Stand

Start out with a strong statement of your position.

John Turner is Canada's most easily forgotten prime minister.

Where's Trudeau when you need him?

Start with a Surprising Fact

All babies are born with blue eyes, or so I've been told.

Start with a Personal Anecdote

When I found out I was pregnant, I confess I had a certain amount of anxiety. I'd killed more than my share of house plants and never had much luck keeping goldfish alive.

Start with the Other Side

Tell what you disagree with and who said it. Give the opposing reasons so that you can later prove them wrong. For examples of this technique, see the editorial or "opinion" page of your newspaper.

The newspaper headlines over the past week give one cause for pause. Urban unemployment is up. Urban crime is up. Urban anxiety is up. Despite these reminders of the downside of urban life, Canada's largest city continues to provide its residents with a high quality of life.

Tell a Brief Story About Someone Else

Give one or two paragraphs to a single typical case, and then make your general point. The brief story makes clear the personal implications of the topic you will present. Magazine articles often use this method.

My neighbours' son is an only child. His parents have from time to time lamented that fact. They have felt the pressure put on parents to offer a sibling to the first-born. Their child is in sharp contrast to the stereotype of an only child. He is generous, not spoiled. He is well-adjusted, not troubled. He is accepting, not demanding. Perhaps it is time for the arguments in favour of the one-child family to be shared, as reassurance and comfort to parents of only children.

Move from the General to the Specific

Begin with the wider context of the topic and then zero in on the case at hand.

When we think of "strength," we usually picture physical strength—for instance, a weight lifter. But there are subtler forms of strength. Perhaps the rarest is moral strength: the ability to do what is right, even when it is inconvenient, unpopular, or dangerous. My grandfather in Italy was actually a strongman in the circus, but I remember him more for his moral strength than for his powerful arms.

Use the News Lead

Write one sentence incorporating *who, what, when, where, how,* and sometimes *why.*

During the 14th century, in less than three years, one-third of Europe's population died of the bubonic plague.

Start with a Quotation

Find a great line from someone else that either supports or conflicts with your selected thesis. Use it as an attention grabber.

All art is a kind of confession, more or less oblique. All artists, if they are to survive, are forced, at last, to tell the whole story; to vomit the anguish up.—James Baldwin

MIDDLES

The body of your essay could be three to many paragraphs long. The introduction has smoothly paved the way for you to make and prove your point.

Each body paragraph is devoted to one main idea. Each offers up specific examples to support the thesis.

The intro and conclusion hold the essay together. The body is what gives your paper substance.

Paragraphs—Long and Short

The paragraphs of your essay lead the reader step by step through your ideas. Each paragraph should make one point, and every sentence in it should relate to that one point. The statement of that point is known as the topic sentence. Usually the paragraph begins by stating the point and then goes on to explain it and make it specific.

Paragraphs should be as long as they need to be to make one point. Sometimes one or two strong sentences can be enough. At other times you need nine or ten sentences to explain your point. However, you want to avoid writing an essay that consists of either one long paragraph or a series of very short ones. Paragraphs give readers a visual landing, a place to pause; so use your eye and vary the paragraph lengths as content demands.

Indent the First Word of the Paragraph

In college or university papers, indent the first word of each paragraph five spaces if you are using a typewriter, or about 1.5 centimetres if you are using a word processor. In business letters or reports, where you single-space between lines, omit the indention and double-space between the paragraphs.

Break Up Long Paragraphs

A paragraph that is more than ten sentences usually should be divided. Find a natural point for division.

- a new subject or idea
- a turning point in a story
- the start of an example
- a change of location or time

Expand Short Paragraphs

Too many short paragraphs can make your thoughts seem fragmented. If you have a string of paragraphs that consist of one or two sentences, you may need to *combine, develop,* or *omit* some of your paragraphs.

Combine —

- Join two paragraphs on the same point.
- Include examples in the same paragraph as the point they illustrate.
- Regroup your major ideas and make a new paragraph plan.

Develop —

- Give examples or reasons to support your point.
- Cite facts, statistics, or evidence to support your point.
- Relate an incident or event that supports your point.
- Explain a general term.
- Quote authorities to back up what you say.

Omit —

If you have a short paragraph that cannot be expanded or combined with another, chances are that paragraph should be dropped. Sometimes you have to decide whether you really want or need to explain a particular point.

Check for Continuity

Within a paragraph, make sure that your sentences follow a logical sequence. Each sentence should build on the previous one and lead to the next.

Link your paragraphs together with transitions, by taking words or ideas from one paragraph and using them at the beginning of the next one.

A Tip

If you keep having trouble with your paragraphs, you can rely on this basic paragraph pattern.

• A main point, stated in one sentence.

• An explanation of any general words in your main point.

• Examples or details that support your point.

• The reason why each example supports your point.

• A sentence to sum up.

CONCLUSIONS

Don't end your paper by merely repeating your thesis or introduction. Don't end it with preaching or clichés or empty
thoughts. Don't end it by contradicting yourself, introducing a
new tangent, or just slowly "turning down the volume." Consider, out of all that you have written, what is most important.
Sometimes you will want to write a quick summary; other times
you will want a longer conclusion that probes your topic more
deeply.

Here are several approaches to writing a conclusion.

Summarize

Stress your main points, but avoid repeating earlier phrases word
for word.

Suggest a Solution to a Problem

Come up with a solution you think might make a difference, and
tell how the information you've presented could affect the future.

Put Your Ideas in a Wider Perspective

What is the importance of what you have said? What is the larger
meaning? Move from the specifics of your topic to the deeper
concerns it suggests.

Raise Further Questions or Implications

Which issues now remain? Acknowledge the limitations of what
you have covered. Reaffirm what you *have* established. Examine
what it implies.

HOW TO WORK ON A SECOND DRAFT

Revision is not just fixing errors. It means taking a fresh look at all aspects of your paper, then moving some parts of it and completely rewriting others. Look at your first draft from the following angles.

The Real Goal of Your Paper

- A big danger is straying from your subject. It's tempting to include good ideas or long examples that are related to your subject but do not support your main point.

- You might find it helpful to write a sentence that begins, "The main point of my paper is ..." This sentence need not go into your paper, but keep it in front of you as you revise to make sure that every detail supports your main point. Note that your *real* point may not be the point you started with. As you look over your work, decide what you are really saying. You may need to write a new introduction that stresses your real goal.

Strong Parts and Weak Parts

- Build up what's good. When we revise, we tend to focus on the weak spots. Instead, start by looking for the good parts in your paper. Underline or highlight them, and write more about them. Add examples. Explain more fully. You may find that you have written a new, much better paper.

- Fix up what's bad. Now look at the parts that are giving you trouble. Do you really need them? Are they in the right place? If you got tangled up trying to say something you consider important, stop and ask yourself, "What is it I'm trying to say, after all?" Then say it to yourself in plain English and write it down that way.

Reading Aloud to a Well-chosen Friend

- Share your work with a friend who is honest, whose opinion you respect, and who has some comfort with language and written expression.

- When you read your paper to a friend, notice what you *add* as you read—what information or explanations you feel compelled to put in. Jot down these additions and put them into the paper.

- Ask your friend to tell you what came through. All you want is what he or she heard—not whether it's good, not how to change it. Then let your friend ask you questions. What did he or she want to know that you didn't share? What didn't he or she understand? Where might it be useful to have more examples and details? Guard against letting your friend take over and tell you what to write. Remember, your essay is uniquely your thoughts, expressed in your individual way.

Final Touches

- Look again at the proportions of your paper. Are some of the paragraphs too short and choppy? Is there one that is overly long? Strive for balance.

- Look at your first and last paragraphs. You may find that your old first paragraph no longer makes your real point. If so, write a new one. Play with the first and last sentences of your paper so that you begin and end with the strongest statements you can. For an important sentence, write the idea three or four different ways—with very different wording—and then choose the best.

- Write a title that catches the reader's attention and that announces your subject.

- Proofread your paper closely several times and make corrections. Watch especially for errors in any of the new material you've written.

HOW TO MAKE A PAPER LONGER (OR SHORTER)

Adding words and phrases to your paper makes it at most a few centimetres longer. Adding new points or new examples makes it grow half a page at a time. There are times when *cutting* a little bit instead makes your whole paper stronger.

How to Make a Paper Longer

- Explain your point, or add an example to demonstrate it—or even add a new point.

- Mention other views on the subject that differ from your own. Either incorporate them (showing the evidence for them) or disprove them (telling why others might accept them and why you reject them).

- Add details (facts, sensory details, events that happened, things you can see or hear). Details are the life of a paper. Instead of writing, "We got something to drink," write, "We swiped a sixpack from Tom's cooler."

- Expand your conclusion: discuss implications and questions that your paper brings to mind.

BUT ...

- Don't add empty phrases, because they make your writing boring. Don't fake length by using fat margins or large type. Don't repeat yourself needlessly.

How to Make a Paper Shorter

- Condense minor points. Sometimes you think a point is necessary, but when you read your paper to a friend, you notice that both of you get bored in that section. Or sometimes you get tangled up trying to make a point clear when you can cover it briefly or cut it entirely.

- Watch your *pace* when you tell a series of events. Head toward the main point or event directly. Don't get lost in boring preliminary details.

- Avoid getting sidetracked. The digression may interest you, but it probably doesn't add to the essay.

TRANSITIONS

Transitions are *bridges* that take the reader from one thought to the next. These bridges link your ideas together and help you avoid choppy writing.

First Check the Order of Your Ideas

If you are having trouble with transitions, it may be that your points are out of order. Make a list of your main points and juggle them into a logical sequence. Then add transitions to underscore the movement from one point to the next.

Use Transition Words

Keep your transitions brief and inconspicuous. Here are some transition words you can use to illustrate certain points or relationships.

adding a point: furthermore, besides, finally, in addition to

emphasis: above all, indeed, in fact, in other words, more to the point, most important

time: then, afterwards, eventually, next, immediately, meanwhile, previously, already, often, since then, now, later, usually

space: next to, across from, above, below, nearby, inside, beyond, between, surrounding

cause and effect: consequently, as a result, therefore, thus, then, so

examples: for example, for instance

progression: first, second, third, it follows that

contrast: but, however, in contrast, instead, nevertheless, on the contrary, on the other hand, though, still, unfortunately, that being said

similarity: like, also, likewise, similarly, as

concession: although, yet, of course, after all, granted, admittedly, while it is true

conclusions: therefore, to sum up, in brief, in general, in short, for these reasons, in retrospect, finally, in conclusion

Use Repetition of Key Words and Ideas

Repeat the word itself or variations of it.

I can never forget the *year* of the flood. That was the *year* I grew up.

Everyone agreed that Iona was *beautiful*. Her *beauty*, however, did not always endear her to others.

Use pronouns.

People who have hypoglycemia usually need to be on a special diet. *They* should, at the very least, avoid eating sugar.

Use synonyms—different words with the same meaning.

When you repot plants, be certain to use a high grade of potting *soil*. Plants need good rich *dirt* in order to thrive.

Use Transitional Sentences Between Paragraphs

Usually the transition between paragraphs comes in the first sentence of the new paragraph.

Even though Hortense followed all of these useful suggestions, she still ran into an unforeseen problem.

Because of these results, the researchers decided to try a new experiment.

Notice that in these examples, the first half of the sentence refers to a previous paragraph; the second half points to the paragraph that is beginning.

PROOFREADING TIPS

Proofreading deserves as much attention as your actual writing. Careless errors can undermine what you have said and cause readers to make negative judgments about you. So make a practice of proofreading several times.

Here are some tips to help you spot mistakes.

Take a Break Between Writing and Proofreading

Always put a little distance between the writing of a paper and the proofreading of it. That way you'll see it fresh and catch errors you might have otherwise overlooked. Set the paper aside for the night (or even for twenty minutes) while you catch your breath. When you write in class, train yourself *not* to write up until the final moment; give yourself an extra ten minutes before the end of class, take a short break, and then proofread your paper several times before handing it in. If you reread your work immediately after writing it, you'll see what you intended to write, rather than what you actually wrote.

Search for Trouble

Assume that you have made unconscious errors, and really look for them. Slow down your reading considerably. Look carefully at every word.

Know Your Own Typical Mistakes

Before you proofread, look over any papers you've already had corrected and received back. Recall the errors you need to watch for. As you're writing your next paper, take ten minutes to learn from the last one. It can be helpful for you to use page 235 at the back of this book as a place to keep track of your usual or repeated errors. This page can act as a handy and accessible reference when you are proofreading future work.

Proofread for One Type of Error

If periods and commas are your biggest problem, or if you always leave off apostrophes, or if you always write *your* for *you're*, go through the paper checking for just that one problem. Then go back and proofread to check for other mistakes.

Proofread Out of Order

Try starting with the last sentence of the paper and reading backwards to the first sentence; or proofread the second half of the paper first (since that's where most of the errors usually are), take a break, and then proofread the first half.

Proofread Aloud

Try always to read your paper aloud at least once. This will slow you down, and you'll *hear* the difference between what you meant to write and what you actually wrote.

Look Up Anything You're Not Sure About

Use this book and a dictionary. Guessing doesn't always work. You'll learn how to avoid errors in the future if you look things up in the present. By taking the time to look it up, you'll develop into a strong, careful, accurate writer.

Proofread Your Final Copy

It does no good to proofread a draft of your paper and then *not* proofread the final paper. Sometimes in the final draft you have corrected an earlier problem but in the process made new errors. This happens often, especially in typewritten papers. Remember that a *typo* is just as much an error as any other error.

With a Word Processor, Proofread on Both Screen and Page

If you are using a word processor, scroll through and make corrections on the screen. Use the spelling checker if there is one, but remember that a spelling checker will not catch commonly confused words like *to* and *too* or *your* and *you're*. You will still need to proofread your printed copy.

PART THREE

MEETING SPECIFIC REQUIREMENTS: SUGGESTIONS ON PRODUCING A WELL-EXECUTED DOCUMENT

- *Format of Written Communication*
- *Writing on Demand*
- *Articles and Personal Essays*
- *Using the Library*
- *Writing Research Papers*
- *Writing About Literature*
- *Technicalities*
- *How to Quote from Your Sources*
- *Plagiarism*
- *Documentation*
- *Sample Paragraph Using Citations*
- *Works Cited*

FORMAT OF WRITTEN COMMUNICATION

Paper

- Use letter-size paper. Do *not* use sticky, erasable paper.
- Use one side of the paper only.
- Staple once or clip in the upper left-hand corner.
- If you use a computer and print out on fan-fold paper, separate the pages and remove perforated edges.

Typeface

- If you have a choice, use 12-point type.
- Do not use all-capital letters or all italics. Since these are nonstandard and not often used, they are more difficult to read.

Spacing

- Double-space between lines.
- Use 3 or 4 centimetre margins on all four sides.
- Indent the first line of each paragraph about 2 centimetres (about five spaces on a typewriter).
- Do not justify your right-hand margin (i.e., give it a straight edge) unless asked to do so. When you do, the spacing between letters and words is distorted, and your paper is harder to read.
- At the bottom of the page, use a full last line unless you're ending a paragraph. It's all right to end a page in the middle of a sentence.

Spacing After Punctuation

- Leave *one* space after all punctuation marks. Never leave two spaces.

- If your keyboard does not allow a dash (—), make one using two hyphens (--).

- To make an ellipsis (...), always use three "tight" periods. Leave a space before the first and after the third.

- Never begin a line with a period or a comma.

- Never put a space before a punctuation mark.

Dividing Words

- As much as possible, avoid dividing words from one line to the next. If a word has five letters or fewer, fit it on one line or the other.

- Divide only between syllables. To find the syllables, look up the word in a dictionary. Syllables are marked like this: *guar•an•tee.*

- Never divide a one-syllable word, like *brought.*

- Never divide a word after only one letter.

Page Numbers

Number every page except the first.

Cover Sheet

The cover sheet should contain these.

- the title, without quotation marks or underlining

- your name

- the date

- the course title and number

- the teacher's name

Centre the title in the middle of the page and put the other information in the lower right-hand corner.

Some Advice About Keystroking

It pays to learn to use a word processor. If you don't own a computer, most colleges and universities and many public libraries have a computer room where you can key in and print out your paper. If someone else does it for you, be sure that person doesn't interfere with the content. Don't let someone else tell you what you mean to say or how to do your assignment.

A Word About Proofreading

If you are using a computer, make regular use of the thesaurus and spellcheck functions. Also, watch out for those errors you already know you are likely to make. It often helps to proofread your paper many times, each time watching for a different error.

No matter who has typed your paper, you must read the typed copy several times. A typo counts as an error; it's no excuse to say, "Oh, that's just a typo."

Often teachers don't mind if you correct your typed copy with a pen. If it's okay, you can draw a line through the word you wish to change and write the correction above the line. Small corrections can also be made with correction fluid. If you use a word processor, proofread your paper both on the monitor and on the printout. Don't rely solely on a spelling checker; it will miss errors like *to* for *too, their* or *they're* for *there, it's* for *its*.

WRITING ON DEMAND

A wave of panic—that's what most people feel when they are handed an assignment to be written on the spur of the moment, whether at work or in class. Some writers, feeling the pressure, plunge in and write the first thoughts that come to mind. But your first thoughts aren't necessarily your best thoughts. There's a more constructive way to write against the clock.

Take Your Time at the Beginning

- Consider the purpose of your writing and read any instructions carefully. Be sure you're fulfilling the requirements of the assignment. Write what you are asked to write, and take time to consider how best to approach the task at hand.

- Jot down notes for a few minutes. Do a scattergram. Be open to what comes. Catch a variety of possible directions. Don't censor yourself, and don't write whole sentences yet—just a word or phrase for each idea, example, or fact.

- Take a few more minutes to expand your notes. Play with the ideas. Have fun exploring different tangents. Stay calm. Don't start writing too soon.

- Decide on the parts of your essay, letter, or report.

- Assign different points to different parts of your piece of writing. Design the shape of the whole.

Stress Organization

In fiction writing—for example, short story writing—you may choose to begin without a clear notion of where the story is going. You just jump in and let the characters take control, so that the story unfolds naturally, and often in a surprising way.

With nonfiction—for example, essay writing—you should plan the piece carefully and exert control over its direction. Instead of letting the essay just roll along, decide on the best placement of each element, each detail, each bit of evidence.

Introductions, Middles, and Conclusions

- Your *introduction* should indicate the parts of your essay. One simple technique is to allow a full sentence in your introduction for each of the main points you plan to make.

  Sigmund Freud is famous for three important ideas. He popularized the idea that we repress or bottle up our feelings. He explored the idea of the unconscious. Most important, he stressed the idea that our family relationships when we are children determine our adult relationships.

  Note how the number "three" in the first sentence helps the reader see the plan of the whole essay. Each of the three points will become a separate paragraph in your essay.

- Now write a paragraph for each point from your introduction. Have a topic sentence in each paragraph that clearly notes the main point of the paragraph. In each middle paragraph, restate the point mentioned in the introduction, explain what you mean by any general words, and give facts or examples to prove your point. Always offer evidence to help readers accept your point of view.

- Your *conclusion* states what you most want the reader to remember.

Reserve Time at the End

- Stop writing at least ten minutes before the end of the allotted time.

- Read your essay for content. Don't add to it unless you find a *major* omission or point of confusion. Late additions usually create errors and disorganization.

- Proofread, with special attention to the second half of the essay (where rushing leads to errors) and to the very first sentence.

Leave yourself enough time to review your work several times. With each review, be mindful of a particular possible error. Check spelling, particularly for your "pet peeve" words and for sound-alike words such as *to* and *too*, *then* and *than*. Check your *periods* to be sure you have no run-on sentences or fragments. Double-check for subject/verb agreement, pronoun antecedent agreement, and tense agreement. Confirm that modifiers are properly located. Be sure you have used the correct parts of speech. Confirm that you have properly chosen your pronouns, prepositions, and transitions. Be sure meaning is clear. Look carefully to make sure you haven't left out any words or letters.

Short Essays on an Exam

For *short essays on an exam*, each answer should consist of one long paragraph. Write a one-sentence introduction that uses words from the question and asserts your answer. Then, in the same paragraph, present three facts to support your answer, explaining one fact at a time. Finally, sum up your position in the last sentence of the paragraph.

ARTICLES AND PERSONAL ESSAYS

Stress What You Have Discovered

For a personal essay, you have many more options. While the three-point essay can get you by, it can easily become stilted and boring. In a personal essay, you need more room to explore your ideas.

- If you can't come up with a strong introduction at first, write your essay and then go back and write an introduction. You may discover a central idea through the process of writing the essay; this idea can then serve as your introduction.

- If you're writing about a significant incident or event in your life, begin your essay by describing the event. Describe it *briefly*, using vivid details to bring it to life. Then use most of your essay to tell what you learned from this event or how it has changed you.

- If you are giving your opinion about a topic, you can sometimes use personal examples to support your position. Begin your essay with a strong statement; make it clear in your introduction where you stand. Use the rest of your essay to argue assertively for what you think is right. Generalizations without support aren't persuasive. What can you offer as proof that your point of view is a just and sensible one?

- Be sure to divide your essay into paragraphs. Make sure each paragraph is full of *specific* examples, facts, or details. Use your own experiences, your own observations, and incidents you've read or heard about.

- In your conclusion, don't moralize or lecture and don't fall back on overused generalizations. Say what matters to you or what you have discovered. Say it in language representative of your own unique style.

Here are some other tips.

Don't Labour over One Difficult Word, Phrase, or Paragraph

- If one part of the paper isn't coming, jump ahead or back and spend time with a part that's easier to write. Once you get on a roll, the previously tricky part will come to you much more easily.

- If you're stuck for one word, leave an obvious blank; return to it later and find that difficult, previously evasive word.

- If you get confused about what you want to say, stop writing for a moment. Say out loud, "What I mean is ..." and write down what comes after. Some people find it helpful to say sentences out loud before committing them to paper.

Don't Start Over

- Stick to your plan. If you get a new idea, use a star sign or an arrow to show where it goes.

- Leave room after each paragraph for ideas you might want to add later. If you are writing in an exam booklet, write on only one side of the page so that you will have room for insertions.

- If you add or cut a main point, go back and revise your introduction to account for the change.

Don't Pad Your Writing

Use a direct, no-nonsense style. Don't try for big words—they just lead to errors when you are under time pressure. Simply state your points and the facts to back them up, one step at a time.

Don't Make a Neat Copy—

Copying over wastes precious time, and the copy tends to be full of slips and errors. Instead, put a line through an error and correct it above the line. Use an upside-down V (^) for a short insertion, a star sign (*) or arrow for a long insertion.

USING THE LIBRARY

When you are searching for information, there's no better place to begin than your local or school library. Many cities also have a central reference library, with access to just about any source you could name. Familiarize yourself with all these resources in your neighbourhood.

Public Access Catalogues and Computerized Catalogues

Most libraries have their card catalogues on a computer and no longer keep the public-access card catalogue up to date. Use the computerized catalogue wherever possible. A librarian can quickly and easily explain to you how to conduct a computer search for any desired information.

Books, media holdings, and reference materials are catalogued by *author, title,* and *subject.* If you don't have a specific author or title in mind, use the subject listing and be prepared to look under several different headings.

Most public and high school libraries use the Dewey Decimal System; most college and university libraries use the Library of Congress Classification System. This system divides all knowledge into twenty-one classes; each class is identified by a letter (or letters) of the alphabet. Each item in the library is assigned a classification letter (or letters) as well as a string of numbers. This letter/number string is the item's *call number.* Every item in the catalogue will have one. You need the complete call number to locate a book. It also helps to copy down the name of both the author and the item. With this information you will be able to find the item you want. You can also scan the shelves nearest that item for other titles relating to your subject of interest.

It can be useful to note the different letters for different subject areas.

A - General works; almanacs, encyclopedias, yearbooks
B - Philosophy, psychology, religion
C - History – auxiliary sciences
D - History – general and Old World

E - History – U.S.A.
FC - History – Canada
G - Geography, anthropology, recreation
H - Social sciences

J - Political science
K - Law
L - Education
S - Agriculture

T - Technology
U - Military science
V - Naval science
Z - Bibliography and
      library science

SPECIFIC EXAMPLES
PE 1628 Dictionaries
PE 1591 Thesaurus
HF 5383 Résumés
HA 202 UF—U.S. statistics
HC 111 M37—Market research handbook

Stacks

These are the rows of books that take up most of the space on
every floor. To find a book you want, you have to have the exact
call number. If the book isn't in the stacks, you can ask at the
circulation desk whether it's checked out. If it is, you can put
your name down to receive it when it's returned.

The Reserve Room

This is the section in the library where you go to check out, for a
few hours or overnight, books and other materials that your
teacher has put aside for the class.

Reference Section

Materials in this section include encyclopedias, dictionaries,
bibliographies, and special collections of information. You can use
them only in the library. Many libraries have copy machines so
that you can reproduce the most pertinent pages for use outside
the library.

Periodicals Section (or index room)

Here you find annual indexes—in bound volumes and, more
recently, on computer—to newspapers, magazines, and journals.
The Canadian Index, the Reader's Guide, and the Magazine Index
list all subjects covered in popular magazines. Other indexes are
more specialized; ask the librarian for help. List the periodicals

and pages you want and check the holdings file, which is the list of magazines your library carries. Often a magazine is available in a bound volume, or you can get a copy from the circulation desk. Many times, especially for newspaper articles, you will have to read copies on microfilm or microfiche.

Microfilm, Microfiche, and CD-ROM

This separate area houses microfilm, microfiche, and CD-ROM. Each slide, roll of film, or disk contains hundreds of pages of newspapers or magazines. Someone is usually there to help you use the machine the first time; after that, it's easy. You can make a copy of any page you want, often on the machine itself.

The Vertical or Clip File

Somewhere in every library is the vertical or clip file, sometimes also known as the pamphlet file. In this file are housed years and years of clippings, accumulations of pamphlets—you find all sorts of information about any subjects the librarians thought important. This is an especially good source of information about your province or hometown.

Media Section

Here you can see slides, filmstrips, and videotapes; listen to records or compact disks; look at slides under microscopes; and listen to foreign language tapes.

Typewriters and Computers

More and more libraries are providing computers on which you can type your paper. Some libraries even offer computer literacy classes.

Two Other Important Services

Interlibrary Loan: At your request, the library can obtain copies of books and photocopies of articles from other libraries.

Computer Searches: For a small fee, you can request a computer search to identify most sources about a subject field. Many libraries now also offer on-line hookups to various databases.

WRITING RESEARCH PAPERS

Many writers feel overwhelmed by that terrifying request for a "research" or "term" paper. Don't be scared—a research or term paper is simply a fairly long paper in which you set forth a point of view and support it with outside references. Here are some methods for keeping control of your paper.

Before Beginning Research, Freewrite About the Topic

To discover your preliminary main point, write down quickly what you already know. Dash down random thoughts nonstop for about fifteen minutes without thinking about organization. You can include the reasons you're interested in this subject and questions you'd like to answer.

Write a Controlling Sentence

Before searching for reading materials, spend some concentrated time writing one sentence that will explain and limit your paper. This sentence is often called a thesis statement or a topic sentence. The point is to limit your focus so that you don't read yourself into a hole, overwhelm yourself with research. You will sometimes have to use several sentences to convey your intention, but where possible, try for one. An example—

Pizza is the most wholesome fast food on the market today.

Search for Supporting Information

The first step is to choose your reading. Go to the library and comb all the resources there. If your subject isn't listed, look under related subjects. You can also ask someone who knows the field for suggestions about what's best to read or who is best to talk to. Look for recent articles. Check bibliographies in the backs of books. It can be exciting to follow the leads you discover as you search for information. Also, don't overlook other sources, such as these—

- local organizations
- interviews with experts in the field
- a visit to an institution

- your family
- your classmates
- local libraries
- businesses

Take Notes from Your Reading

After you've written down a few key questions, focus your reading on answering those questions. Remember that you want to gather supporting information, not copy other people's words. Be aware that you cannot write your paper while taking notes. These must be two separate steps.

- First, write down the details about your source that you will need for your Works Cited page.

for a book: author, title, place of publication, publisher, and date of publication

for an article: author, title of article, title of publication, date, and pages

Keeping an index card for each source with all this information is a good idea; that way, when you type your Works Cited you can simply rearrange the cards in alphabetical order.

- Next, take notes *sparingly* as you read. Take notes in phrases, not whole sentences. You will drive yourself crazy if you try to take down every word. It's best to read a number of paragraphs, then summarize them in your own words. Immediately write the source (author's last name and page number will do it). If a quotation strikes you as especially strong or interesting, copy it word for word and put quotation marks around it in your notes. Be accurate in noting the page number, since you'll need to let the reader know precisely where you found your information.

(A word about photocopying material: if you find something very valuable, photocopy it to save time. But immediately write on the photocopy the publication information so that you don't forget where it came from.)

- As you read, if you get an insight of your own, stop and write about it. Remember, this paper should be written by a human being—you—and you need to develop your own opinions and thoughts about your subject.

- After you've finished taking all your notes, go back over them and mark all the important points with an asterisk or with a highlighting pen. You might also find it helpful to make a brief outline or a short summary for each of your sources.

- It can be helpful to have an assortment of highlighters in different colours, so that you can highlight sections according to where the research should go in the essay: blue for body paragraph number one, green for body paragraph number two, and so on. It can also be useful to have separate file folders for each paragraph of your essay. Put research into a different folder—that is, for each point of your opening thesis.

Discover Your Own Perspective

- After you have read and understood your sources, put your notes, books, and magazines aside in order to find your own position.

- Spend time freewriting, making a scattergram, or listing ideas until you know what you think about the topic.

- Go back to the sentence you wrote before you began your research—the controlling idea. Is this still your main point? Is it focused, original, meaningful, and supportable? Does the question posed hold interest for you? If not, develop a new thesis.

Organize Your Material

- Without consulting your notes, develop a short, informal outline—all the major points you plan to make, put into a logical arrangement. Some writers use the paper tape from an adding machine to plot out their story, article, essay, letter, or report. Others use recipe cards and a cork board. Work out a general shape for your essay, before deciding where the points from your research work best. Develop a short, informal outline.

- Still without consulting your notes, just from memory, write a paragraph about each topic in your plan.

- Now you can consult your notes. Read them and see which notes relate to the main points on your list. You may remember a main point you can add to your list. See if particular quotations and facts you discovered during your research fit with any of your main points, but don't feel you have to fit in everything you've found. And don't feel you must shift the direction of your essay to include a piece of unrelated information. Write a paragraph about each topic in your plan. Where possible, lead in to an appropriate bit of research.

- Avoid the temptation to have your quotations and paraphrased materials determine the content of your paper. The essay should already have its shape and direction. The research provides the supporting evidence, not the body of the essay. The research is a secondary element, not a primary one.

Now Write Your Essay

- Don't lose sight of your audience, intention, and thesis. Let these three guide your writing.

- Don't use fancy words and long sentences. Tell what you know and what you want to say, stressing what is most important. Decide on your style and tone. What will make your work memorable and distinctive? What attitude do you want to take with it? What emotional response would you like to draw from the reader?

- Write to persuade. Remember that *you* are the authority. Your job is to convince the reader of your view of the topic. Use the facts you have found to back up your position; support your position with every sentence you write.

- Anticipate the reader's questions and doubts and respond to them ahead of time.

Incorporate Your Sources into Your Paper

- Avoid merely giving a part of your paper to each source you read; instead, give a part to each of the points you want to make.

- Select from your notes only the support you need for your own points. Eliminate material that does not pertain to your main points.

- Use your sources to expand each of your points. State each point and explain it with material from your research. Every time you use an opinion or fact originating with someone else, give credit to your source in parentheses.

- After presenting quotations or facts, make it clear how they relate to the point of your paragraph.

Vary the Way You Use Your Sources

There are three main ways of presenting information: *direct quotation, paraphrase,* and *summary.*

- *Direct Quotation*

  This is the most common method—and the one most often overused in papers. Avoid relying too much on quotation by making a conscious effort to use the other two methods: *paraphrase* and *summary.* Your paper should not be more than 15 percent direct quotations. They are best used for memorable or distinctive phrases.

  In direct quotation, you use the *exact* wording from your material, inside quotation marks. Even if you use only a phrase or a key word, you must use quotation marks to indicate that it has been taken from another source.

  If the quoted material is lengthy (more than four lines of another author's work), don't use quotation marks. Instead, indent the block an extra two centimetres (three or four spaces).

  The sections "Quotation Marks" and "How to Quote from Your Sources" offer further help in using quotations correctly.

- *Paraphrase*

  When you paraphrase, you take someone else's ideas or facts and put them into your own words. Usually you paraphrase one statement, not more than a few lines, at one time. A good time to paraphrase rather than quote directly is in telling basic facts: dates, statistics, places, and so on. The pitfall of paraphrasing is that you can't half do it; that is, if you mix in some of the author's exact words, you must use quotation marks around them.

- *Summary*

When you summarize, you take a substantial amount of material and condense it. You can summarize a long passage, several pages, a chapter, or even an entire article or book. Use summary when you want to acknowledge a conflicting idea or when you want to cover a related idea without too much detail.

Whether you have used word-for-word quotations, paraphrased, or summarized the source material, be sure to identify the source (author or key title word) and the page number in parentheses immediately after presenting the material. The three examples below are taken from the same source, to show how you can vary the way you use your sources.

Word-for-Word Quotation

1. *The Shipping News* breaks with convention by having sentence fragments throughout. "Not his fault. Not to be stuffed away in some back room or left to cast and drool about the streets like in the old days. Things could be done" (Proulx 145–146). These snippets suggest each character's internal dialogue, and the pace at which ideas fly in.

Indented Block, Word-for-Word Quotation

2. *The Shipping News* breaks with convention by having sentence fragments throughout.

> Here was a sudden subject for Wavey. Down's syndrome, she said, and she wanted the boy to have a decent life. Not his fault. Not to be stuffed away in some back room or left to cast and drool about the streets like in the old days. Things could be done ... (145–146)

These snippets suggest each character's internal dialogue and the pace at which ideas fly in.

Summary

3. *The Shipping News* breaks with convention by having sentence
    fragments throughout. E. Annie Proulx frequently does away with
    naming the subject or specifying the verb. She abbreviates the
    thought, breaking it down to its most basic and central components
    (145–146). These snippets suggest each character's internal dia-
    logue and the pace at which ideas fly in.

Revise Your Essay

Copying over a first draft is not the same as revising. Careful
revision requires several steps.

*   Take the time to make sure that you have written clearly—not
    in an artificial style.

*   Be sure each paragraph has one clear point and is logically
    connected to the paragraphs before and after it.

*   Omit or move information that doesn't fit with a paragraph's
    main point.

*   Look for places where the reader will need more information in
    order to follow your point.

*   Check for smoothness in the transitions into and out of direct
    quotations, paraphrases, and summaries.

Edit Your Essay

Use *Rules of Thumb,* Parts Four and Five, to make corrections
before you type. The proofreader's checklist at the back of this
book will prove useful. Make necessary changes to promote
correctness, accuracy, and clear meaning. Also proofread the final
copy, since new errors can occur when you are doing the final
draft.

WRITING ABOUT LITERATURE

How to Think Through Your Essay

When you are asked to write about literature—let's say it's a novel—you will need to be certain of your teacher's expectations. Some teachers want a *summary* of the novel in which you tell the main points of what you've read and then give an evaluation. But most teachers want you to go past that, to the more challenging stage of *analysis*. Your reader wants your essay to do more than retell the tale. In your paper you should stress an important idea in the novel and demonstrate what gave you that idea.

Omit Plot Summary and the Author's Life

A summary condenses the plot of a novel and retells it in brief. Biographical information gives details of an author's life: place and date of birth, upbringing, education, employment, relationships, work published, successes and frustrations.

Unless you've been asked to, don't include a detailed plot summary that repeats all the points of the novel or the author's life story. The reader wants to hear your analysis and your take on the novel. A reader who is interested only in plot could simply read the novel.

Gather Your First Impressions of the Topic

Begin by freewriting about the question you have been asked or the topic you are considering. Write your first impressions quickly, without pausing, to get your ideas on paper. Do not worry about organization yet; don't even stop to review your notes. After ten minutes, read your ideas, underline the most important ones, and write a sentence to sum up your main idea.

Review the Text

Search for evidence to support your main idea, and also for evidence that might lead you to modify it. The evidence could include incidents in the story or subtleties of style. Make notes as you review and mark passages to quote.

Organize Your Essay

Look at your original freewriting and revise your main idea if necessary. Decide on the parts of your idea and on the order that will make those parts clear.

Use Evidence to Back Up Your Points

Writing that "it was a good story" doesn't tell the reader anything. You must offer evidence to *prove* it was a good story. For each main point you make, offer details from the novel to support the point. In some cases, briefly quote the author. After referring to a detail or quoting a passage, always explain why that detail or passage supports your point.

Avoid generalities and vague statements. Instead, always seek out specific lines, details, and moments that help you prove your point.

Write a Title for Your Paper

Since your title is the reader's first contact with your work, it should create interest and motivate the reader to read on. The title should express the main idea of your paper, not just give the title of the text.

TECHNICALITIES

Titles

<u>Underline</u> titles of books, plays, magazines, and newspapers, or set them in *italics*. Put "quotation marks" around titles of stories, articles, poems, and television shows. As a general rule, use italics or underlining for the title of an entire, long piece; use quotation marks for parts of a whole—for elements contained within an anthology, collection, magazine, or paper—or for shorter works.

Authors

Use the author's full name the first time you mention it. Thereafter, use the full *or* last name—not the first name by itself.

> Pauline Johnson wrote three collections of poetry, one volume of tales, and one novel.

or

> Johnson wrote three collections of poetry, one volume of tales, and one novel.

Identifying the Title and Author

Be sure to identify the title and author early in your essay, even if you've already done so in your title.

> In "The Song My Paddle Sings," Johnson ...
> "Dinner Along the Amazon" by Timothy Findley is ...
> Freud's *The Interpretation of Dreams* ...

Note carefully the punctuation in these examples.

Verb Tense

Use the present tense to refer to the action in a work of literature.

> The speaker of the poem longs for his youth.

> Early in the novel, Elizabeth misjudges Darcy.

Crediting Your Sources

Citations can take various forms. The one described in this reference guide is one of the most common in present-day use.

- If you are quoting from only one source, give information about the edition you used at the end of the paper. List the author, the title, the city of publication, the publisher, and the copyright date. If you want to provide the original date of publication, put it immediately after the title.

Fitzgerald, Zelda. *Save Me the Waltz*. 1932, New York: NAL, 1960.

Metcalf, John. *Adult Entertainment*. Toronto: Macmillan, 1986.

- Directly after each quotation, give the page number in parentheses.

The novel ends with a couple "watching the twilight" (203).

- For a poem (such as Coleridge's "Rime of the Ancient Mariner") give the line numbers.

Water, water, everywhere,
And all the boards did shrink;
Water, water, everywhere,
Nor any drop to drink. (119–122)

- For the Bible, give the title of the specific book, with chapter and verse.

To every thing there is a season, and a time to every purpose under the heaven. (Eccles. 3.1)

- For a play (such as Shakespeare's *Antony and Cleopatra*), give act, scene, and lines.

Age cannot wither her, nor custom stale
Her infinite variety. (II.2.234–235)

- For more than one source, see "Documentation."

HOW TO QUOTE FROM YOUR SOURCES

A good quotation demonstrates the point you are making.

Keep the Quotations Secondary to Your Own Ideas and Words

Your essay shouldn't be wall-to-wall quotations; instead, your own words and thoughts should be supported by quotations from the work and from others. Each quotation should illustrate a point you are making. Quotations are not filler; rather, they are proof that what you're saying is supportable. Before and after the quotation, stress your point.

Don't Use Many Quotations

Too many quotations chop up your paper and lead the reader away from the points you are making. Most of the time, tell what you have learned in your own style. Instead of quoting, you can *summarize* (give the main points of what you read) or *paraphrase* (explain a single point in detail in your own words).

Keep Your Quotations Brief

Short quotations are the easiest and most graceful to use. Avoid using many quotations of over three or four lines. If you want to use a long quotation, omit sections that do not apply, using ellipses (...) to indicate the parts you've left out. A long quotation should be followed by a discussion, in the same paragraph, of the points you are making about the quotation.

Indent Lengthy Quotations

At times, a longer quotation is preferable or necessary. To make it easy for the reader to see where the quotation starts and ends, set off the quoted material in an indented block.

In an interview with Claudia Tate, Alice Walker talked about her responsibility to her audience:

> Had I ever written a story with all white characters? Well, of course I have. Years ago I wrote a wonderful story which I must find, if it's not packed in a trunk somewhere back in Brooklyn. It's a good story, and I know I'll publish it one day. But at the time I wrote it, nobody would buy it because it was a very chilling view of white people, of these particular white people. I had written what I saw. I had written what I thought. I had written what I felt, but this was a view that was totally unacceptable to everyone. Nobody wanted this particular view. (in Geddes 882)

Introduce Your Quotations

Direct quotations should usually be preceded by identifying tags. Always make clear who is speaking and the source of the information.

> Marie-Claire Blais says, "I only made it through because of the unconsciousness of youth" (in Geddes 90).

There are various ways of incorporating the author's name and any other pertinent information into the text. For variety's sake, use more than one way in your essay.

> Dr. Trey Porter, an authority on adolescent psychology, maintains that all teenagers share a major fantasy: "They all dream of the day they will be free from parental control."

As a general rule, don't begin a sentence or a paragraph with a direct quotation without an introduction.

Incorporate Each Quotation into a Clear Sentence

Be sure your quotations make sense in terms of both content and sentence structure. If you use fragments of quotations, weave them into complete sentences.

> Photographer Michael George states that "wasting film" ultimately saves a photographer time and effort.

PLAGIARISM

If you use the ideas or specific words of others without giving credit, you are committing plagiarism. It is a form of cheating or stealing. When you plagiarize, readers can easily mistake other people's ideas for your own. Plagiarism involves *using other people's facts or opinions without identifying your sources; or using someone else's words without acknowledging that you have done so.*

The penalties for plagiarism can be severe: loss of credibility, damage to one's reputation, failure of a course, and even expulsion from college or university. Unintentional plagiarism is still plagiarism, so be careful—learn and follow the rules.

To Avoid Plagiarism

- When in doubt, always give credit for a fact, quotation, or opinion taken from a book or other source. This is true even when you use your own wording.

- When you use another writer's wording—even a phrase— always put quotation marks around the writer's exact words.

- Write with your books closed. Do not write with a book or magazine open next to you. Don't go back and forth taking ideas from a source and writing them into your paper.

- Don't let your sources take over the essay. Tell what you know well in your own style, stressing what you find most important. Have confidence in what you have to say. That way there's no need to rely on the source to say it for you.

DOCUMENTATION

Documentation involves noting clearly where someone else's ideas or words begin and end, and giving enough information about your sources for those ideas or words that the reader could go directly to them.

Some of you may have learned the footnote/endnote/bibliography system of giving credit. In this system, quoted material was numbered 1, 2, 3, and so on; each number referred the reader to either the bottom of the page (footnote) or the end of the paper (endnote) for complete information about the source.

This system complicated life for typists, who had to estimate how much space to save at the bottom of the page—a frustrating task. Also, the same information had to be typed over and over and over again. It was also somewhat frustrating for readers, who had to look to the bottom of the page or to the end of the paper to find out who said what.

Footnotes and endnotes are used less often in modern writing. Nowadays, the preferred method of documenting sources is to add two elements to a paper: citations, and a list of works cited.

Citations

When you give citations in a paper, you tell specifically where you got a piece of information—in other words, the *source* you used.

When to Give Your Source

You must acknowledge in your paper the source of these.

- a direct quotation
- a statistic
- an idea
- someone else's opinion

- concrete facts

- information not commonly known

Even if you *paraphrase* (put someone else's words into your own words) or *summarize* (condense someone else's words or ideas), you still must acknowledge the source of your information.

If a fact is common knowledge (Pierre Trudeau was a Liberal prime minister, two negatives make a positive, water boils at 100 degrees), you don't have to attribute the information to a source.

How to Use Parenthetical Citation

The current method for citing sources is *parenthetical citation*. In this system you give your source in parentheses immediately after you give the information. Readers can then find the complete source at the end of your paper in Works Cited.

In the body of the essay, there must be enough information that readers can find the reference in Works Cited. In Works Cited, there must be enough information that readers can go and find the same sources you used in writing your essay.

The three most common citations are these.

- author and page number

- title and page number

- page number only

This brief information tells the reader what the source is. It also acts as a legend, referring the reader to complete source information at the back of the paper.

Author and Page Number

Put the author's last name and the page number in parentheses immediately after the information.

(Waters 297)
(Metcalf 7)

Notice that there is no "p." and no comma. In the text it looks like this.

> The best olive oils "often have a greenish cast" (Waters 297).

> Charis tries to comfort herself by quietly chanting "You pay your fare, you cross, you drink of the River of Forgetfulness" (Atwood 61).

If your citation comes at the end of a sentence, the period goes *outside* the last parenthesis. (Exception: With indented block quotations, the period goes *before* the parentheses.)

Title and Page Number

Often articles, editorials, pamphlets, and other reading matter have no author listed. For example, a document produced by the government won't note who wrote the information. Corporations as well often fail to credit those who write their articles, newsletters, or pamphlets. In such cases, give the *first* distinctive word of the title, followed by the page number.

> A recent survey compared frozen pizzas for taste and texture ("Frozen" 330).

If more than one work by the same author is being referred to or discussed in your essay, you must note key words from the title so that the reader can easily tell which of the author's works the material was taken from.

If you have named the writer in the body of the text, you need only mention the title, or part of the title. If the source author hasn't been named, you will need to identify the writer within the citation.

> (*Survival* 87).
> (*Surfacing* 112).

> (Atwood, *Survival* 87).
> (Atwood, *Surfacing* 112).

> (Glover, *Dog Attempts,* 23).
> (Glover, *A Guide to Animal Behaviour,* 11).

Page Number Only

Renaming the author isn't necessary when it is already clear who the source of the information is. Put only the page number in parentheses when you have already mentioned the author's name.

> Regina Schrambling says that the Tex-Mex flavour is "welcomed by most Americans" (125).

> Audrey Thomas's character Francine "found herself pushing her hair back all the time, so that the waitress, at least, would see she wore a wedding ring" (206).

When possible, use this method of citation. Mentioning the author's name as you present information makes your paper more cohesive and readable.

Special Cases

• *Secondhand Quotations*
When you quote someone who has been quoted in one of your sources, use *in* (as in "quoted in").

> Julie Wilson, who says her food is "fresh and honest," makes a blue cheese and pear pizza (in Claiborne and Franey 69).

In this example Wilson said it, although you found it in Claiborne and Franey. Note that Wilson will not be listed in Works Cited; Claiborne and Franey will be.

> Timothy Findley says that "it's vicious being a writer" (in Geddes 257).

In this example Findley said it, although you found it in Geddes.

• *Interview or Speech*
If your source is an interview, lecture, or speech, you have two choices: include the person's name in your paragraph and use no parenthetical citation; or note the speaker's name in parentheses after the quoted, paraphrased, or summarized material. You can give details about the interview or speech in Works Cited.

(Schoemperlen).

• *Two Sources by the Same Author*
When you have two or more sources by the same author, use the
first major identifying word to indicate the title of the work
you're citing.

> Claiborne prefers to chop the mozzarella rather than grate it
> (*International* 440).

or

> Some chefs prefer to chop rather than grate the mozzarella
> (Claiborne, *International* 440).

• *Organization as Author*
Sometimes the author is an organization.

> According to Agriculture Canada, one slice of plain pizza has 145
> calories (22).

or

> One slice of plain pizza has 145 calories (Agriculture Canada 22).

How Often to Give Citations

When several facts in a row in one paragraph all come from the
same page of a source, use one citation to cover them all. Place
the citation after the last fact, but alert the reader at the outset
with a phrase such as "According to Janet O'Toole ..."

Do not, however, wait more than a few lines to let the reader
know where the fact came from. The citation must be in the same
paragraph as the fact.

Remember that you must give citations for information, not just
for quotations.

SAMPLE PARAGRAPH USING CITATIONS

From the paragraph below you can see how various citations are used. (You will rarely have this many citations in one short paragraph.)

> When the first pizzeria opened in New York City in 1905 ("Pizza" 490), it introduced the classic Italian pizza—bread dough covered with tomato sauce and cheese. Now, almost a century later, pizza is one of North America's favourite foods. In addition to the classic version, pizza lovers can take their pick of thin or thick crust, all-white pizzas, vegetarian pizzas, or even more exotic experiments. For example, there is Tex-Mex pizza, a taste Regina Schrambling points out is "welcomed by most" (125), and there is the French pissaladière, which adds fresh herbs, black olives, and anchovies (Child 151). Julie Wilson, who calls her food "fresh and honest," offers a high-brow combination: pizza made with blue cheese and pears (in Claiborne and Franey 70).

WORKS CITED

When you were gathering your material, you may have used a "working bibliography," a list of potential sources. Now that you have written your paper and have seen which sources you actually used, you must compile a Works Cited page for the end of your paper.

There are four major points to understand about a Works Cited page.

- List only those sources that you actually referred to in your paper.

- List the whole article, or essay, or book—not just the pages you used.

- Alphabetize your list of sources by the authors' last names. If no author is listed, alphabetize by the first main word in the title.

- Format is extremely important, although admittedly there is more than one acceptable format. The main thing is to be consistent within the format you choose. Pay special attention to order, spacing, and punctuation.

  — Put the author's last name first.

  — Double-space the entire list.

  — Start each entry at the left margin so that it is easier for readers to spot the author's last name.

  — Indent the second and third lines of each entry.

  — Use periods to separate the items in a citation.

  — Put a period at the end of each entry.

Specific Entries

Book. Author. *Title*. City: Publisher, date.

Glover, Douglas. *A Guide to Animal Behaviour*. Fredericton: Goose Lane, 1991.

Richler, Mordecai. *Joshua Then and Now.* Toronto: McClelland & Stewart, 1980.

Shoemperlen, Diane. *Hockey Night in Canada and Other Stories.* Kingston: Quarry Press, 1991.

Waters, Alice. *Chez Panisse Menu Cookbook.* New York: Random House, 1982.

Article in a Magazine

Author. "Title of Article." *Title of Periodical.* Date:page(s).

Hancock, Geoff. "Cheap Sex and Sudden Death." *Canadian Fiction Magazine: Sex and Death.* No. 73. 1991:4–6.

Marto, Nancy. "Jane Urquhart." *Blood and Aphorisms* 19. Summer 1995:37–41.

Schrambling, Regina. "Tex-Mex Pizza." *Working Woman.* February 1988:125.

Article in a Newspaper

Author (if given). "Title of Article." *Title of Newspaper.* Complete date, section:page(s).

Chapman, Geoff. "Youth Blows Impressive Horn." *Toronto Star.* July 19, 1995:D3.

"Pillsbury's Pizza Unit to Be Sold." *New York Times.* March 18, 1988:D1,7.

Encyclopedia

"Title of Article." *Encyclopedia.* Year of the edition.

If the author is known, list that as well. If the reference isn't well known, include the city and publisher as well. It isn't necessary to include the page number, since the topic areas are organized alphabetically.

"Pizza." *Encyclopaedia Britannica: Micropaedia.* 1986 ed.

Thomas, Clara. "Laurence, Margaret." *The Canadian Encyclopedia.* Edmonton: Hurtig, 1988 ed.

Article, Poem, or Story in a Collection or Anthology

Author of article. "Title of Article." *Title of Book*. Editor of book. City: Publisher, date. Pages covered by article or story.

Atwood, Margaret. "Hairball." *The Art of Short Fiction: An International Anthology*. Ed. Gary Geddes. Toronto: HarperCollins, 1993. 20–30.

Cook, Joan Marble. "Italy: Myths and Truths." *Italy*. Ed. Ronald Steel. New York: Wilson, 1963. 31–37.

Ondaatje, Michael. "The Gate in His Head." *The New Canadian Anthology: Poetry and Short Fiction in English*. Ed. Robert Lecker and Jack David. Scarborough, Ont.: Nelson, 1988.

Special Cases

• *No Author Listed*

Use the first main word of the title and alphabetize according to that.

"Frozen Pizza." *Consumer Reports*. May 1986: 327.

• *Two or More Authors*

Give the last name first for the first author only; use first name first for the other author(s).

Anderson, Jean, and Ruth Buchan. *Half a Can of Tomato Paste and Other Culinary Dilemmas*. New York: Harper, 1980.

Katsavos, Anna, and Elizabeth Wheeler. *Complements*. New York: McGraw-Hill, 1995.

Klaus, Carl, Chris Anderson, and Rebecca Faery. *In Depth: Essayists for Our Time*. Orlando: Harcourt Brace Jovanovich, 1993.

If four or more authors, name only the first, followed by "et al." (Latin for "and others").

- *Additional Works by the Same Author*

Use three dashes and a period in place of the author's name and alphabetize the works by title.

Claiborne, Craig. *Craig Claiborne's New York Times Video Cookbook.* Videocassette. New York Times Productions, 1985. 110 min.

———. *New York Times International Cookbook.* New York: Harper, 1971.

Shoemperlen, Diane. *Hockey Night in Canada and Other Stories.* Kingston: Quarry Press, 1991.

———. *The Man of My Dreams.* Toronto: Macmillan, 1990.

- *Pamphlet*

Follow the format for a book. Often an organization is the publisher. Sometimes no author is listed.

- *Radio or Television Program*

Put quotation marks around the title of the program. Give the network, if any, then the station call letters and city. Then list the date of the broadcast.

"Kids in the Hall." CBC, Toronto. September 10, 1994.

"New York and Company." WNYC, New York City. April 10, 1991.

"Winsday." CKY TV, Winnipeg. April 6, 1980.

- *Videocassette*

List the author or director and the producer, the release date, and the running time.

Claiborne, Craig. *Craig Claiborne's New York Times Video Cookbook.* Videocassette. New York Times Productions, 1985. 110 min.

- *Recording*

List the group or recording artist, the title of the piece, the company label, the catalogue number, and the date.

Cochrane, Tom. *Mad Mad World.* Capitol, C2-597723, 1991.

• *Interview*

Give the person's name and position, the kind of interview (personal or telephone), and the date.

O'Reilly, Kevin [Owner, O'Reilly's Pizza Parlour]. Personal Interview. October 19, 1992.

Schoemperlen, Diane. Personal Interview. July 24, 1993.

• *Lecture*

Give the speaker's name, then the title of the speech, sponsor of the lecture, location, city, and date.

Egoyan, Atom. Lecture. Film Institute. Algonquin College, Ottawa, July 1985.

Urquhart, Jane. Lecture. Kingston School of Writing. Queen's University, Kingston, July 1991.

A sample of a Works Cited page follows on page 111. It illustrates a variety of sources and therefore is longer than you probably will need. The facing page identifies the category of each source.

Explanations of Works Cited

Book with two authors.

Pamphlet, unsigned, no date.

Cartoon in a weekly magazine, untitled.
Multiple authors of book, one volume cited.

Videocassette (use this form for audio or computer works).

Repeated author; same author as above.
Repeated author with first citing of co-author; newspaper article.

Single article from an edited collection (use this form for an essay or story in an anthology).

Magazine article (monthly), unsigned.
Organization as author, two volumes with both volumes cited, organization as publisher.

Radio program (use this form for a television program).

Interview (use this form for a lecture or speech).

Newspaper article, unsigned.

Encyclopedia article, unsigned.
Magazine article (monthly), signed.

Book with a single author.

Government Publication.

Works Cited

Anderson, Jean, and Ruth Buchan. *Half a Can of Tomato Paste and Other Culinary Dilemmas.* New York: Harper, 1980.

Browning Microwave Oven Cooking Guide. Mahwah, NJ: Sharp Electronics Corporation, n.d.

Cheney, Tom. Cartoon. *New Yorker.* January 30, 1989:69.

Child, Julia, Louisette Bertholle, and Simone Beck. *Mastering the Art of French Cooking.* Vol. 1. New York: Knopf, 1966.

Claiborne, Craig. *Craig Claiborne's New York Times Video Cookbook.* Videocassette. New York Times Productions, 1985. 110 min.

———. *New York Times International Cookbook.* New York: Harper, 1971.

Claiborne, Craig, and Pierre Franey. "Feasts Against Frost." *New York Times.* January 17, 1988, Sec. 6:69–70.

Cook, Joan Marble. "Italy: Myths and Truths." *Italy.* Ed. Ronald Steel. New York: Wilson, 1963. 31–37.

"Frozen Pizza." *Consumer Reports.* May 1986:327+.

Gourmet. *The Gourmet Cookbook.* Rev. ed. 2 vols. New York: Gourmet, 1965.

"New York and Company." WNYC, New York City. April 10, 1991.

O'Reilly, Kevin [Owner, O'Reilly's Pizza Parlour]. Personal Interview. October 19, 1992.

"Pillsbury's Pizza Unit to Be Sold." *New York Times.* March 18, 1988:D1,7.

"Pizza." *Encyclopaedia Britannica: Micropaedia.* 1986 ed.

Schrambling, Regina. "Tex-Mex Pizza." *Working Woman.* February 1988:125.

Waters, Alice. *Chez Panisse Menu Cookbook.* New York: Random House, 1982.

U.S. Dept. of Agriculture. *Nutritive Value of Foods.* Washington: GPO, 1981.

PART FOUR
CORRECTNESS

- *A Word About Correctness*
- *Parts of Speech and Sentence Parts*
- *Sentence Fragments and Run-on Sentences*
- *Verb Agreement*
- *Shifting Verb Tenses*
- *Tangled Sentences*
- *Correct Pronouns*
- *Consistent Pronouns*
- *Vague Pronouns*
- *Avoiding Other Mechanical Problems*
- *Who, Whom, Which, That*
- *Confusing Words*
- *One Word or Two?*
- *Spelling*
- *Capitals*
- *Abbreviations and Numbers*
- *Commas*
- *Semicolons and Colons*
- *Periods, Exclamation Marks, and Question Marks*
- *Dashes and Parentheses*
- *Hyphens*
- *Other Punctuation Marks*
- *Apostrophes*
- *Quotation Marks*

A WORD ABOUT CORRECTNESS

It's not wise to violate the rules until you know how to observe them.

T.S. Eliot (in Winokur 5)

Too much concern about correctness too early in the process of writing can inhibit your writing; too little concern can come between you and your readers. Don't let the fear of errors dominate the experience of writing for you. On the other hand, we would be misleading you if we told you that correctness doesn't matter. Basic errors in writing will distract and turn off even the most determined readers. Basic errors can also negatively affect your reputation: a reader may decide you are careless, or lacking in knowledge, or worse. We encourage you to master these few rules as quickly as possible so that you can feel secure about your writing. Once you are, you'll be free to concentrate on what you want to say.

PARTS OF SPEECH AND SENTENCE PARTS

Different words perform different functions in a sentence. When you understand each part of speech and sentence part, you can be sure you are using your words, phrases, and clauses correctly.

• *Adjectives*
Describe or add information about nouns or pronouns: *beautiful, new.*

> Her new dress is beautiful.
> He drives a beautiful car.

• *Adverbs*
Describe or add information about verbs, adjectives, or other adverbs (usually end in *-ly*): *beautifully, newly.*

> The newly cleaned carpet smells beautifully fresh.
> She dances beautifully.

• *Appositives*
Rename a nearby noun or pronoun (use a comma before or after): *my grade three teacher.*

> Mr. Smythe, my grade three teacher, ended up moving in next door.

• *Articles*
Help qualify or define nouns: *a, an, the.*

> The boy brought a bat and an orange ball to the park. His brother brought hockey cards and a hoop with him, but said it was too great an honour to even touch the cards, let alone let his brother play with them.

• *Conjunctions*
Join words, phrases, clauses, sentences: *and, but, or, nor, for, so, yet* (with comma); *however, therefore, moreover, furthermore, nevertheless* (with semicolon).

Jane and John have worked for the same company for five years; however, now that they're getting married, John has decided to change companies.

Shelley bought a dog, but her husband is terribly allergic to it.

• *Gerunds*
The "-ing" form of a verb; used as a noun: *walking, waiting, leaning.*

Learning Spanish wasn't as easy as she'd hoped.
Thinking is easier than doing.

• *Interjections*
Show surprise, emotion: *Oh! Really! Hah!*

No! You can't take money from my wallet.
Wow! That's a good deal.

• *Nouns*
Name a person, place, or thing (capitalize specific names): *cat, Mars, beauty, thing.*

Their cat, Mars, is a beauty. She looks like a cartoon cat. She's really something to see.

• *Objects*
Receive the action of the verb: *book, me.*

He gave the book to me.

• *Prepositions*
Give information about time, place, direction, relationship: *about, above, across, after, before, below, by.*

The cousin of the twins walked across the stream and over the hill.

• *Pronouns*
Take the place of nouns: *I, you, he, she, who, whom, whose, it, we, they, me, you, him, her, hers, its, our, ours, their, theirs, this, that, these, those, anyone, anybody, anything, both, each, either, everybody, every-one, everything.*

Gail said she'd give me a ride. I'm counting on it.

• *Subjects*
The *who* or the *what* involved in the action or the state of being of the sentence: *I, you, he, she, who, it, we, they, book.*

> The book is a good one. They loaned it to me.

• *Subordinating Conjunctions*
Introduce a subordinate clause, and give information about its relationship to the rest of the sentence. Fragments occur when a subordinate clause isn't linked to a dependent clause. Beware of fragments when you use these words—

after, although, as because, before, even if, how, if, in (case, order that, that), now that, once, provided that, since, so that, supposing that, than, that, though, unless, until, when, where, whether, while, why

> If I were you, I'd call him right back.

• *Verbs*
Express action or state of being: *to be, to feel, to have, to walk, to jump.*

> I am happy to be here. I feel somewhat tired from having walked so far.

Word-carpentry is like any other carpentry: you must join your sentences smoothly.

Anatole France (in Winokur 9)

SENTENCE FRAGMENTS AND RUN-ON SENTENCES

To correct both sentence fragments and run-on sentences, you need to know what a complete sentence is.

Often you reach a pause in your writing and wonder, "Do I put a comma or a period?" The length of a sentence has nothing to do with the right choice. Instead, it depends on whether your thought is complete or needs to connect with something else to make sense.

Fragments can be a problem because only a portion of the thought is made clear by the writer. Readers are left to complete the thought for themselves. This demands too much of the reader and can lead to misinterpretation.

Writing has laws of perspective, of light and shade, just as painting does, or music. If you are born knowing them, fine. If not, learn them. Then arrange the rules to suit yourself.
                                    Truman Capote (in Winokur 5)

You will come across fragments in your reading. Advertisements are full of them because they're punchy, fast paced, and often contemporary.

New! Improved! For silky soft hair!

Poetry is often a series of fragments. Short stories employ fragments as a stylistic device and in naturalistic dialogue. People speak in fragments all the time.

Because I said so.
Maybe.
After the party, before I went home.

In a formal essay, fragments are to be avoided because they can confuse or frustrate your readers.

Run-on sentences can also be confusing, because there is too much information in one sentence to be easily understood or absorbed.

> On Saturday, after I'd been to Doug's party, I ran into Bill and Ted and we all decided to go for a burger some place and we got into his car, Ted's I mean, we went for a little spin, and got lost along the way because he never did have a very good sense of direction and I was getting hungrier and hungrier because I hadn't had any lunch I hadn't eaten since breakfast probably eight o'clock or so and there we were, barrelling down the highway, away from the city, totally in the wrong direction for any kind of food and nobody seemed to notice we were going the wrong way except for me probably because I was so absolutely starving Ted ran out of gas we were out there miles from nowhere and all I could think of was how hungry I was.

A writer must group thoughts together so that the reader can spot what relates to what. It exhausts the reader when one sentence is too full of information.

Again, we speak in run-ons all too often. Fiction writers sometimes use them as an attention grabber or stylistic tool; in formal writing, avoid them. When you come to the end of a complete and independent thought, put in a period, exclamation mark, or question mark as appropriate.

RECOGNIZING COMPLETE SENTENCES

• A sentence always has a *subject* and a *verb*.

> I won.
> Phillippe snores.
> This soup is cold.

I, Phillippe, soup are the subjects; *won, snores, is* are the verbs. Notice that the verb enables the subject to *do* or *be* something. These very short sentences have only a one-word subject and a one-word verb.

- Sentences can have more than one subject and more than one verb.

  Tracy and Pete have a new home.
  They bought an old house and restored it.

- Sometimes the subject is understood to be "you," the reader. This type of sentence is usually a command or a direction.

  Avoid submerging this product in water.
  Walk two blocks past the traffic light.
  Run!

- Usually a word or phrase completes the subject and verb.

  Janeen eats three apples a day.
  Suzanne spent all of her savings.
  Grasshoppers are lazy.
  This is my latest fiancé.

Variations

- Sometimes a word or group of words introduces the main part of a sentence.

  However, the bar is closed.
  Therefore, we are planning a trip to the moon.
  For example, Mona screams when she talks.
  Then she threw three straight strikes.
  At the end of the game, the referee and the goalie got into a fight.
  In the cabin by the lake, you'll find the paddles and life jackets.

- Sometimes two short complete sentences are joined by a comma and connecting word or by a semicolon.

  Janeen eats three apples a day, but she also eats junk food.
  She spent all her savings, and now she is filling her credit cards.
  Grasshoppers are lazy; they are not very hard to catch.

- Sometimes a sentence has two parts: the main part (a complete short sentence) and a *subordinated* part (a complete short sentence preceded by a *subordinating* word such as *because, although, if, when, after,* or *while*). This subordinated part makes no sense outside the rest of the sentence.

I feed my goldfish when I get home.
Suzanne spent all her savings because her brother is ill.

Notice in the first sentence that *I feed my goldfish* could be a complete sentence. On the other hand, *when I get home* is not complete by itself. In the second sentence, *because her brother is ill* is also incomplete when it stands alone.

The two parts of each sentence are reversible.

When I get home, I feed my goldfish.
Because her brother is ill, Suzanne spent all her savings.

RECOGNIZING SENTENCE FRAGMENTS

Many sentence fragments appear to be complete sentences but have elements that make them incomplete.

- A subordinating word in front of a sentence creates a fragment.

fragment: Although Janeen eats three apples a day.

You can fix this fragment by dropping the subordinating word or by connecting the fragment to the sentence before or after it.

correct sentences: Janeen eats three apples a day. *or* Although Janeen eats three apples a day, she still has to see her doctor. *or* Janeen still has to see her doctor although she walks five kilometres a day.

Here are the most common subordinating words; these dependent clause clues always start the incomplete part of a sentence.

after	that
although	though
as, as if	unless
as long as	until
as soon as	what, whatever
because	when, whenever
before	where, wherever
even if, even	whereas
if	whether
in order that	which, whichever
provided that	while
since	who, whom, whose
so that	

A subtle point: Watch out for *and*. Putting *and* between a fragment and a sentence doesn't fix the fragment.

still a fragment: Although Janeen eats three apples a day and she still sees her doctor.

correct sentence: Although Janeen eats three apples a day and she still sees her doctor, she is not yet healthy.

• Certain verb forms cannot serve as the main verb of a sentence. Watch out for verbs ending in *-ing*. Without a helper verb (am, was), a verb ending in *-ing* either is incomplete or is being used as a noun (a person, place, or thing).

incorrect: The boys ran toward the ocean. Leaping across the hot sand.

incorrect: I love walking in the evening and taking in nature's beauty. The sun setting over the prairie. The wind blowing the tall grass.

One solution is to connect the fragment to the preceding sentence.

correct: The boys ran toward the ocean, leaping across the hot sand.

correct: I love walking in the evening and taking in nature's beauty— the sun setting over the prairie and the wind blowing the tall grass.

The second solution is to change the *-ing* verb to a complete verb.

correct: They leaped across the hot sand.

"To" verbs (*to be, to feel*) also often begin fragments.

incorrect: I went back home to talk to my father. To tell him how I feel.

incorrect: Keep this hairdryer away from the sink. To avoid submersion in water.

Reading your work aloud can help you hear an incomplete thought.

To avoid submersion in water ...

You can hear that these words are begging a completer. They are leading naturally into something that isn't present. Fix these fragments by connecting them to the sentence before or after or by adding a subject and verb.

correct: I went back home to talk to my father, to tell him how I feel.

correct: I went back home to talk to my father. I needed to tell him how I feel.

correct: Keep this hairdryer away from the sink to avoid submersion in water.

correct: Keep this hairdryer away from the sink. You must avoid submerging it in water.

"To" verbs and "-ing" verbs *can* begin sentences if a complete verb comes later.

correct: Leaping across the hot sand hurts my feet.

correct: Talking to my father always calms me down.

• A repeated word can create a fragment.

incorrect: Elizabeth's the ideal cat. A cat who both plays and purrs.

incorrect: I am tired of this. Tired of waking up to rain every day.

Often, the best solution here is to replace the period with a dash.

correct: Elizabeth's the ideal cat—a cat who both plays and purrs.

correct: I am tired of this—tired of waking up to rain every day.

- Professional writers sometimes use sentence fragments for emphasis or style. Be sure you have control over fragments before you experiment. In the right place, fragments can be a very powerful device.

Checklist for Recognizing Sentence Fragments

Check sentences that start with subordinating words.

Check sentences with *to* or *-ing* verbs.

Check for the repetition of a word from the end of the previous sentence.

Check for these words, which rarely begin sentences: *such as, especially, not, like, just like, the same as.*

Check for these words, which begin questions but rarely begin other kinds of sentences: *which, who, whose, how, what.*

Proofread your work by reading aloud backwards. Read the last sentence first, then the second-last sentence, then the third-last sentence, and so on. Sometimes it is easier to spot an error when you isolate the sentence from the one it naturally follows.

RECOGNIZING RUN-ON SENTENCES

With a run-on sentence, you have two complete sentences but only a comma between them, or no punctuation at all.

run-on: I went to Gorman's Ice Cream Parlour, I ordered a triple hot fudge sundae.

run-on: Suzanne spent all of her savings now she is flat broke.

There are five ways to fix a run-on.

- Put a period between the two sentences.

  I went to Gorman's Ice Cream Parlour. I ordered a triple hot fudge sundae.
  Suzanne spent all of her savings. Now she is flat broke.

- Put a semicolon between the two sentences.

  I went to Gorman's Ice Cream Parlour; I ordered a triple hot fudge sundae.
  Suzanne spent all of her savings; now she is flat broke.

- Put a comma and a conjunction or joiner word between the two sentences. Some conjunctions are *and, but, so, yet, for, or,* and *nor.*

  I went to Gorman's Ice Cream Parlour, and I ordered a triple hot fudge sundae.
  Suzanne spent all of her savings, so now she is flat broke.

- Use a subordinating word with one of the sentences.

  I went to Gorman's Ice Cream Parlour for a triple hot fudge sundae.
  Because Suzanne spent all of her savings, now she is flat broke.

- Change or take out words so that part of the sentence can no longer stand on its own.

  I went to Gorman's Ice Cream Parlour for a triple fudge sundae.
  Suzanne, having spent all of her savings, is now flat broke.

The two most common spots where run-ons occur are these.

- When a pronoun begins the second sentence.

  Tabby was running around the yard. She fell into a hole.
  The light floated toward us. It gave an eerie glow.

Note that *she* and *it* begin new sentences.

- When *however* begins the second sentence.

  > She says she loves me. However, she doesn't show it.

However and *although* are often used for similar purposes, but they need different punctuation.

  > Suzanne spent all of her savings. However, her rich aunt is helping her out.
  > Suzanne spent all of her savings although she didn't buy anything excessive.

VERB AGREEMENT

Each sentence must have someone or something (the subject) involved in some action or state of being (the verb). The subject must match the verb in number. If the subject is singular, the verb must also be singular. If the subject is plural, the verb must be plural.

Verb Forms

The verb of a sentence expresses action (*walk, talk, laugh*) or a state of being (*be, become*).

The following act as helping verbs, not as main verbs. They express whether an action is possible, probable, necessary, or obligatory.

can	will	should
may	could	would
shall	might	must

She *can* visit the east coast. (is able)
She *should* visit the east coast. (is obliged)
She *may* visit the east coast (it's possible)

The following can be either helping or main verbs.

be, am, is, are, was, were, being, been
do, does, did
have, has, had

"to be"—

• Present tense.

I am	We are
You are	You are
He, she, it is	They are

• Past tense.

I was	We were
You were	You were
He, she, it was	They were

"to have"—

• Present tense.

I have	We have
You have	You have
He, she, it has	They have

• Past tense.

I had	We had
You had	You had
He, she, it had	They had

Regular verb forms—

"to walk"—

• Present tense.

I walk	We walk
You walk	You walk
He, she, it walks	They walk

• Present progressive.

I am walking	We are walking
You are walking	You are walking
He, she, it is walking	They are walking

• Past tense.

I walked	We walked
You walked	You walked
He, she, it walked	They walked

• Present perfect.

I have walked	We have walked
You have walked	You have walked
He, she, it has walked	They have walked

• Past perfect.

I had walked	We had walked
You had walked	You were walked
He, she, it had walked	They had walked

• Past progressive.
(Expresses a continuing action)

I was walking	We were walking
You were walking	You were walking
He, she, it was walking	They were walking

•Future tense.

I will walk	We will walk
You will walk	You will walk
He, she, it will walk	They will walk

• Future progressive.

I will be walking	We will be walking
You will be walking	You will be walking
He, she, it will be walking	They will be walking

Irregular verbs are listed at the end of this book.

MATCHING SUBJECT AND VERB IN NUMBER

Take care when matching your verb to your subject. The word before the verb is not always its subject. Look for *who* or *what* is doing the action. Be able to separate the main parts of the sentence from the phrases that are there only to add information and interest.

- Remember that two singular subjects joined by *and* (the bird *and* the bee) make a plural and need a plural verb. If you substitute a pronoun for the noun or nouns and read the sentence aloud, your ear will hear the correct verb.

  The bird and the bee make music together.
  They [plural] make music together.

- Sometimes an insertion separates the subject and verb. If you read the sentence aloud without the insertion, your ear will hear the correct verb.

  The drummer, not the other musicians, sets the rhythm.
  The drummer … sets the rhythm.

  The lady who sells flowers has a mysterious voice.
  The lady … has a mysterious voice.

- Sometimes an *of* phrase separates the subject and verb. To hear the correct verb, read the sentence without the *of* phrase.

  One of the guests is a sleepwalker.
  One … is a sleepwalker.

  Each of us owns a Wurlitzer jukebox.
  Each … owns a Wurlitzer jukebox.

  The use of cigarettes is dangerous.
  The use … is dangerous.

- The subject of the sentence follows *there was, there were, there is, there are.* You can easily choose the correct verb by rearranging the sentence without the word "there."

  There was one cow in the field.
  One cow [singular] was in the field.

There were two cows in the pasture.
Two cows [plural] were in the pasture.

- Words with *one* and *body* are singular.

anyone, anybody
someone, somebody
everyone, everybody

- However, a multitude is treated as one unit and requires a singular verb.

Everyone except for the twins was laughing.
Somebody always overheats the copying machine.

Collective Nouns

A collective noun is treated as singular if the members of the group are acting as one body or unit rather than as individuals. Nouns to watch for include these.

audience	crowd
class	family
club	jury
committee	team
couple	troop

- Choose a singular verb if you can picture the group as involved in a unified action.

My family eats crowder peas.
The team argues after every game.
A thousand dollars is a lot of money to carry around.
The jury is reaching a decision as we speak.

- Choose the plural form if you can picture the individual members of the group doing their own thing, independently of the other group members.

The family are splitting up and moving all over the globe.
The team are getting into their uniforms.
The jury are back in their homes and regular lives for the weekend.
Dollars are floating out the window, this way and that.

- *-ing* phrases are usually singular.

  Dating two people is tricky.
  Being over six feet tall is hard for some women.
  Leaning over the balcony makes me dizzy.

SHIFTING VERB TENSES

Decide whether past, present, or future tense is most appropriate for your piece. Often you find yourself slipping back and forth between present and past. Try to be consistent, especially within each paragraph. If you change tenses, have a reason for it.

- Use the present tense for writing about literature.

  Scarlett comes into the room and pulls down the draperies.
  Hamlet cannot make up his mind.

- Use the simple past tense to tell your own story or stories from history.

  I lied to the vice-principal.
  Chrétien waved from the top step.

had

Watch out for *had*: you often don't need it. Use *had* to refer to events that were already finished when your story or example took place—the past before the past you're describing. To check, try adding *previously* or *already* next to *had*.

  In 1986 we moved to Vancouver. We had lived in Calgary for three years, and Winnipeg before that.
  If I had known the wheel was loose, I would have stopped.

would

Most of the time, you can leave out *would*. Use it for something that happened regularly during a period of the past.

  The teacher would always make us stand up when she entered the room.

Use *would* for hypothetical situations, in which assumptions are made for the sake of argument.

  If I were you, I would apologize right now.

could/can

Use *could* to refer to the past and *can* to refer to the present.

past: Frank couldn't go in the ocean because it was too rough.

present: Frank can't swim in the ocean because it's too rough.

Use *could* to show what might happen and doesn't; use *can* to show ability.

> My parents make good money. They could buy us anything, but they don't.
> My parents make good money. They can buy us anything we want.

Note: Avoid ungrammatical expressions such as *I seen* and *He has went*. Use *gone, eaten, done, seen, written* after a helping verb.

We went.	We have gone.
I ate.	I have eaten.
He did it.	He has done it.
He saw the light.	He has seen the light.
She wrote well.	She has written a play.

TANGLED SENTENCES

In speech we often say things that, if they were taken literally, wouldn't make much sense. However, listeners are relatively forgiving and usually don't choose to embarrass us for our errors. When we write, the errors are more glaring, since they are there in black and white to be read again and again. Proofread your work carefully, to be sure your meaning is clear. Look at your sentences to make sure the parts belong together and are in the correct sequence.

PARALLEL STRUCTURE

In your sentences, single words should be balanced with single words, phrases with phrases, clauses with clauses. Look at your sentences and spot any words or groupings of words that don't match the others.

Balance parallel ideas linked with coordinating conjunctions (*and, but, or, nor, for, so, yet*). In the same way, balance parallel ideas linked with correlative conjunctions (*either/or, neither/nor, not only/ but also, both/and, whether/or*). The parts of a list (or pair) must be in the same format.

not parallel: I love swimming, to play tennis, and baseball.

parallel: I love swimming, tennis, and baseball.

parallel: I love to swim, to play tennis, and to play baseball.

not parallel: To reach the camp, Marty paddled a canoe and then a horse.

parallel: To reach the camp, Marty paddled a canoe and then rode a horse.

DANGLING OR MISPLACED MODIFIERS

Read the next four sentences carefully. They are all incorrect.

While still in diapers, my mother showed my sister how to swim.
Flying over Galiano Island, the water shone brilliantly.
After walking for hours, the old homestead loomed in the distance.
He held his baby, now sleeping peacefully, after going up to bat.

Modifiers give you more information about someone or something in the sentence. There are two possible problems: dangling modifiers and misplaced modifiers. In the first, a word (often a pronoun) has been left out so that the introductory phrase doesn't fit with what follows.

dangler: Dashing wildly across the platform, the subway train pulled out of the station.

Dashing wildly is attempting to describe something that isn't named in this sentence. As written, it sounds as if the subway train dashed across the platform. To correct it, add the missing word—in this case, *we*—that the modifier is intending to describe.

correct: Dashing wildly across the platform, we saw the subway train pull out of the station.

correct: As we dashed wildly across the platform, the subway train pulled out of the station.

The second problem occurs when a phrase or word in a sentence is too far from the part it goes with.

misplaced: A former athlete, the reporters interviewed Terrence Harley about the use of steroids.

A modifier is supposed to describe the closest noun. Since *the reporters* is positioned next to the modifier, it sounds as if the reporters are a former athlete. To correct a misplaced modifier, move it next to the thing it is describing.

correct: The reporters interviewed Terrence Harley, a former athlete, about the use of steroids.

MIXED SENTENCE PATTERNS

Sometimes you start with one way of getting to a point, but one of the words slides you into a different way of making it. The two patterns get mixed up. Correct a mixed sentence pattern by sticking to one or the other pattern.

mixed (incorrect): By opening the window lets in fresh air.

Here the phrase *opening the window* took over.

correct: By opening the window, I let in fresh air.

correct: Opening the window lets in fresh air.

Read your whole sentence aloud to make sure the end goes with the beginning.

mixed (incorrect): In the Republic of Cameroon has over 200 local languages.

correct: The Republic of Cameroon has over 200 local languages.

correct: In the Republic of Cameroon, over 200 local languages are spoken.

CORRECT PRONOUNS

The following are subject pronouns (i.e., they can be the subject of a sentence).

1st person	I	we
2nd person	You	you
3rd person	he, she, it, who	they, who

The following are object pronouns (i.e., the person or thing *receiving* the action).

1st person	me	us
2nd person	you	you
3rd person	him, her, it, whom	them, whom

Pairs: My Friends and I / My Friends and Me

With a pair of people, try the sentence without the other person.

My friends and I went to the movies.

(... *I* went to the movies, not ... *me* went to the movies. *Me* cannot be the subject of the sentence.)

Carter gave the tickets to my friends and me.

(Carter gave the tickets to *me*, not to *I*. *I* cannot be the object of the sentence.)

The same rule goes for *him, her, he, she*.

We sued her father and her.
(We sued *her*, not We sued *she*.)

Note: Put yourself last in a list.

My friends and I ...
Beverly baked a pumpkin cake for Noah and me.

Don't be afraid of *me*; it's often right.

Between you and me, Mickey is heading for a fall.

(Not Between you and *I*.)

Don't use *myself* when *me* will do.

Sam did the typing for Toby and me.

(Not ... for Toby and *myself*.)

Comparisons

Use *I, he, she, we, they* when comparing with the subject of the sentence—usually the first person in the sentence.

Phil was kinder to Sarah than I was.
John is sweeter than she is.

Sometimes *is* is left off the end.

John is sweeter than she.

Use *me, him, her, us, them* when comparing with the receiver, the object, of the sentence—usually the person mentioned later in the sentence.

Phil was kinder to Sarah than to me.

Note the difference—

He was nastier to Ramona than I.

(He was nastier to Ramona than *I was*.)

He was nastier to Ramona than me.

(He was nastier to Ramona than *to me*.)

who/whom

Who versus *whom* poses a dilemma for many writers. Choosing becomes easier if you visualize the action. Picture a field with two people and a ball in it. One person throws the ball. Another is hit by it. *Who* is the originator of the action, the person throwing the ball. *Whom* is the object of the sentence, the receiver of the action, the one passively standing in the field to get hit by the ball. *Who* writes a letter; *whom* receives it. If you can see which person or thing is the source of the action (the active one) and which person or thing is the receiver of the action (the passive one), you'll be able to choose correctly.

The following sentence may make it easier to remember the distinction.

Who wrote the letter to whom?

Who, the subject, is creating the action. *Whom*, the object, is merely receiving it.

Use *whom* after prepositions such as *to, of, for, from,* and *with.*

For whom were these roses intended?

Use *who* for subjects of verbs.

Who goes in before me?

CONSISTENT PRONOUNS

Be consistent with your pronouns. Don't shift from *a person* to *they* to *you* to *I*. Avoid writing sentences like this.

I got mad; it does make you feel upset when people don't listen.

or

A young person has to be diligent if they want to get ahead.

The words *a person* and *someone* can lead to awkward writing and create errors.

If a person is strong, they will stand up for themselves.
I know someone rich, and they are not very happy.
Everyone should wash their hands before eating.

Note that *a person, someone,* and *everyone* are singular; *they* is plural. Instead of *a person, someone,* or *everyone,* use *people* (which fits with *they*).

If people are strong, they will stand up for themselves.

Better yet, use a true-life example, a real person.

My cousin Marc is strong; he stands up for himself.

A real example makes the grammar correct, and is also much more interesting and memorable. *A person* and *someone* are nobodies.

he, she, I, you, one, we, they

The old-fashioned choice to go with *a person* is *he*.

If a person is strong, he will stand up for himself.

But using *he* presumes that *a person* is male; this choice should be avoided because it could be considered sexist. *He or she* is possible, but not if used several times in a row; when repeated, *he or she* becomes clunky and awkward.

> If a person is strong, he or she will stand up for himself or herself whenever he or she can.

Avoid *he/she* and *s/he*. The best solution, usually, is to use plurals such as *people* and *they*.

> Strong people stand up for themselves.

Don't be afraid of using *I*. It is very strong for writing about emotions and experience. In these matters, being *objective* is not as good as being *truthful*. As Thoreau said, "I should not talk so much about myself if there were anybody else whom I knew as well." Remember that you don't need phrases like *I think* or *in my opinion* because the whole paper is, after all, what *you* choose to say.

You is good for giving directions and writing letters. For essays, it may seem too informal or preachy.

> If you're strong, you stand up for yourself.

Try *we* instead when you mean *people in general*.

> If we are strong, we stand up for ourselves.

In any case, be careful not to mix pronouns. Instead of writing this—

> Riding my bicycle is good for your legs.

Keep the pronouns consistent by writing this—

> Riding my bicycle is good for my legs.

One means *a person*—singular. If you use it, you must stick with it.

> If one is strong, one stands up for oneself.

One is an option for solving the *he/she* problem; it is appropriate for formal writing. But when repeated too often, *one* can sound stuffy. How many times can one say *one* before one makes oneself sound overwhelmingly repetitious?

We can be used to mean *people in general.*

> If we are strong, we stand up for our rights.

Be careful that you mean more than just yourself. Using *I* might be more appropriate.

They is the best solution to the *he/she* problem, but remember that *they* must refer to a plural, such as *many people* or *some people.*

> If people are strong, they stand up for themselves.

Note that "themself" is not a word. Use *themselves,* which is the plural of *himself/herself.*

Often you can avoid using a pronoun entirely. Instead of this—

> A young person has to be diligent if he or she wants to get ahead.

Write this—

> A young person has to be diligent to get ahead.

VAGUE PRONOUNS

Certain pronouns—*which, it, this, that,* and *who*—must refer to a single and easily identified word, not to a whole phrase.

which

Which causes the most trouble of the five. Don't overuse it.

imprecise: Last week I felt sick in which I didn't even get to go to school.

precise: Last week I felt sick. I didn't even get to go to school.

precise: Last week I had a cold which kept me from going to school.

In the last example, *which* clearly refers to *cold*.

Use *in which* only when you mean that one thing is inside the other.

The box in which I keep my jewellery fell apart.

it

When you use *it*, make sure the reader knows what *it* is. *It* is often weak at the start of a sentence, when nothing is being referred to.

imprecise: Eleanore ate a big Chinese dinner and then had a chocolate milkshake for dessert. It made her sick.

precise: Eleanore ate a big Chinese dinner and then had a chocolate milkshake for dessert. The combination made her sick.

this

This cannot refer to a whole situation or a group of things, so insert a word after *this* to sum up what you are referring to.

imprecise: She never calls me, she's never ready when I pick her up for a date, and she forgot my birthday. This makes me angry.

precise: She never calls me, she's never ready when I pick her up for a date, and she forgot my birthday. This neglect makes me angry.

that

That refers to things.

The car that I bought Wednesday is already in the shop.

who

Use *who*—not which—when referring to people.

incorrect: The runner which finished last got all the publicity.

correct: The runner who finished last got all the publicity.

incorrect: The friend which I met at camp called me yesterday.

correct: The friend whom I met at camp called me yesterday.

AVOIDING OTHER MECHANICAL PROBLEMS

The use of language shifts and changes with the passage of time. An essay written in the mid-1990s will differ in word choice, sentence structure, punctuation, style, and tone from one written in the 1890s. Much of what is acceptable in writing today would have been negatively judged as nonstandard even a few years ago.

The following are still worth avoiding; many of your readers could consider them glaring and unacceptable errors.

SPLIT INFINITIVES

An infinitive is the word *to* plus a verb: *to read, to laugh.* Not so many years ago, it was considered a grave error to have any word appear between *to* and its verb.

incorrect: to openly read, to loudly laugh

Nowadays one must consider whether there is anything to be gained by *not* splitting the infinitive.

awkward: To understand my brother really, you would have had to live with my family.

awkward: Really to understand my brother, you would have had to live with my family.

better: To really understand my brother, you would have had to live with my family.

unnecessary: These file folders will help you to effectively organize your research.

better: These file folders will help you to organize your research effectively.

Place a word between *to* and its verb if it adds emphasis, makes sense, and avoids awkward phrasing.

DOUBLE NEGATIVES

The negatives include *no, not, nor, neither, none, never, no one, hardly,* and *scarcely.* Just like in math, two negatives make a positive. If you use more than one in a sentence, readers may find it difficult to figure out what you mean. The safest approach is to avoid using more than one negative in the same clause.

> She never has no money.

The above sentence actually means *she always has money.* If that is what you mean, it would be easier on the reader if you phrased it in the positive. If you "mean" a negative, you need to rephrase so that only one negative word is in the sentence.

> She never has any money.
> She's always without money.

double negative: He hardly never pays me back.

corrected: He always pays me back.

or

> He hardly ever pays me back.

PREPOSITIONS AT THE END OF SENTENCES

Some readers will have been taught to "never end a sentence with a preposition." Certainly, that is often good advice. When you're writing, avoid placing a preposition at the end of the sentence unless the alternative sounds overly formal or awkward.

awkward: That is the man with whom I'd like you to speak.

better: That is the man I'd like you to speak with.

better yet: I'd like you to speak with that man.

unnecessary: That is the hotel I suggest you check into.

better: I suggest you check into that hotel.

unnecessary: Here's the essay I worked on.

better: I worked on this essay.

EMPTY PREPOSITIONS

In speech, we often use unnecessary prepositions. In writing, cut out any word that serves no purpose.

Where did my bank book go [to]?
I couldn't help [from] laughing over the face you made.
Your house is opposite [of] mine.
Uncle Dan fell off [of] the wagon again.

UNANSWERED QUESTIONS

You, as the writer, know what you intend to say. Sometimes you will find it difficult to review your own work with a fresh pair of eyes, without being blinded by what your intentions were. In some cases readers may not be sure what you're talking about. When you are proofreading, be sure your reader has all necessary information.

I ran into Bill, Tom, and Ted at the party. We took his car. He drove, but it would have been far better if he'd let one of the others drive. He lost his licence a month ago. When the police stopped us, suddenly he was pushed behind the wall. You should have seen the look on his face.

The above is an exaggeration of how confusing it can be when references aren't clear. Be sure you've made it easy for the reader to receive your intended meaning.

The final decisions were a shock to the campaign managers, and they have postponed the next meeting.

It's unclear whether *they* refers to the decisions or to the managers. Rephrase so that there can be no misinterpretation.

The final decisions were a shock to the campaign managers, so Mr. Gruff and Ms. Bentley postponed the next meeting.

MIXED METAPHORS

A metaphor is an implied comparison between two different things. Metaphors are jarring to the reader when you use two in close proximity that bear little relation to each other.

The best defence is offense, and you know very well a bird in the hand is worth two in the bush.

These two clichés don't make any sense together.

Milking their sympathy for all she was worth, she squeaked her complaint to her audience.

Here, the first part of the sentence suggests a cow, the second suggests a mouse. Keep the references consistent, related.

COMPARISONS

Some words cannot logically be used in comparisons. For example, *unique* means one of a kind. It is impossible to say that one person is more unique than another.

Another problem can arise if a comparison is introduced but not completed.

It is a longer way. (longer than what?)
Michael has more nerve. (more nerve than whom?)

WHO, WHOM, WHICH, THAT

These four words regularly frustrate the writer. Remember that who (subject) and whom (object) refer to people.

> Eva, who doesn't seem to need much sleep, has plenty of time for reading.
> Nick, to whom I must give thanks, caught the glass bowl just in time.

Which should stand for a specific noun in most situations. It should be separated from the word before it with a comma. *Which* is never used to refer to people.

That has greater flexibility and can refer to people, animals, or things.

> Cats, which many people prefer to other pets, do not like most dogs.
> Cats that chase dogs are not very common.

As a general rule, use *which* for nonrestrictive clauses (i.e., those that aren't essential to the meaning of the sentence and can easily be separated out) and *that* for restrictive clauses (i.e., those that offer essential information).

> The ceramic bowl, which I bought at a craft shop, looks great on my dining room table. (information about the bowl's source is incidental)
> The ceramic bowl that I bought at this shop looks great on my table. (information about the source identifies exactly what bowl)

> The avocado, which is beside the bananas in the fruit basket, is getting too ripe. (information about the avocado's location is incidental)
> Avocado is one ingredient that I like to have in my salads. (information about the avocado is essential to the sentence)

Sometimes *that* isn't necessary in a sentence. At other times it must be there for the sentence to make sense.

> She said she wanted to see me today.
> She said that she wanted to see me today.

In the above case, *that* doesn't make much difference to the sentence.

The coach said last game saves were dramatically up.

In this example the meaning is unclear when *that* is left out.

The coach said that last game saves were dramatically up.
The coach said last game that saves were dramatically up.

CONFUSING WORDS

These words are used all the time, so you need to know them. Find the ones that give you trouble and learn them.

a, an —

Use *a* before words starting with consonant sounds or long *u*.

a bat, a cat, a hat, a hard place, a union

Use *an* before words that start with vowels or that are pronounced as if they did.

an age, an egg, an igloo, an office, an ugly dog, an hour, an M&M

accept, except —

Accept is a verb meaning to take or receive. *Except* means not including.

I never accept collect phone calls.
Everybody except Tina laughed.

affect, effect —

Affect is a verb meaning to change or influence. *Effect* is almost always a noun that means result or consequence.

Starlight affects us in ways we don't understand.
We are studying the effects of starlight on human beings.

etc. —

This is an abbreviation of the Latin *et cetera*, which means "and so forth." It is always followed by a period. Don't write *and etc.* Many good writers don't use etc.; instead, they write out the list of things *etc.* refers to.

We bought confetti, serpentine, fireworks, etc., for the party.

good, well—

Good is an adjective that describes a noun or pronoun. *Well* is an adverb that describes a verb, adjective, or other adverb. Try your sentence with both. If *well* fits, use it.

incorrect: We were delighted that Ben had done so good on his test.

correct: We were delighted that Ben had done so well on his test.

Leo plays Trivial Pursuit well.

(*Well* gives more information about the verb, *plays*.)

Leo is a good player at Trivial Pursuit.

(*Good* gives more information about the noun, *player*.)

But note these tricky cases.

Olivia looks good. (She's good-looking.)
Rivka looks well. (She's no longer sick.)
Clara sees well. (Her eyes work.)

it's, its—

It's is a contraction meaning "it is." *Its* is the possessive of "it."

It's easy.
Every goat is attached to its own legs.

lay, lie—

Even the most careful writers often confuse these. *Lay* means "to put something down" and always refers to an object. *Lie* means "to rest on a surface" and is always attached to a preposition. Note that once you *lay* something down, it *lies* there. It's a good idea to consult your dictionary every time you use one of these verbs, to make sure you are using the correct form of the correct verb.

She is laying the cards on the table.
He laid the cards on the table.

(*Cards* is the object of *lay*.)

I like to lie down in the afternoon.
Yesterday I lay down for half an hour.

(The prepositions attached to *lie* are *in* and *for*.)

loose, lose—

Loose means not tight. *Lose* is a verb meaning to misplace or be defeated.

After he lost fifteen kilos, his jeans were all loose.
I constantly lose my glasses.
I win; you lose.

no, new, now, know, knew—

No is negative; *new* is not old; *now* is the present moment. *Know* and *knew* refer to knowledge.

of, have—

Note: *could have, should have, would have*—or *would've*—not *would of*

passed, past—

You can *pass* a course, a car, a football, and so on; you can also *pass away* (die). *Past* means "yesterday" or "beyond."

Kirtley passed me on the street; he passed English this term.
The coach passed away.
He can never forget his past romances.
You can't live in the past.

quiet, quit, quite—

Watch how you spell these—they mean very different things.

He is the quiet type.
Sal quit her job the day she won the lottery.
The monkeys are quite noisy today.

than, then—

Than is used for comparisons. *Then* usually means next.

I'd rather dance than eat.
She then added a drop of water.

their, there, they're—

Their is the possessive of "them." *There* generally refers to a place or points to an idea. *They're* is the contraction for "they are."

You hurt their feelings.
There are two very good reasons why you should go there.
They're hard to handle.

to, too, two—

To implies a direction; it is also part of a verb. *Too* can mean "very" or "also." *Two* is the number before three.

Give it to me. Go to Vancouver if you need to find her.
It's too hot. For you, too?
Two of us are staying here.

were, we're, where—

Were is the past tense of "are." *We're* is the short form of "we are." *Where* refers to a place.

We were happier then.
We're as silly as we can be.
Where were you?

whether, weather—

Whether means "if" or refers to alternatives. *Weather* is what you see outside the window.

Ask whether you can go.
Whether you go or not, I'm staying.
The weather is too cold for swimming.

who's, whose—

Who's is the short form of "who is." *Whose* is the possessive of "who."

Who's coming with us?
Whose diamond is this?

woman, women—

Women means more than one *woman*.

This woman is different from all other women.

your, you're—

Your is the possessive of "you." *You're* is the short form of "you are."

That is your problem.
I'd like to know what you're thinking.

ONE WORD OR TWO?

a lot—

I owe you a lot—a whole lot.

(*A lot* is always written as two words. Some readers find it a bit casual.)

all ready, already—

We were all ready for Grandpa's wedding.
Helen already has plans for Saturday.

all right—

It's all right with me if you want to quit.

a long, along—

Childhood seems like a long time ago.
Come along to the carnival.

a part, apart—

I want a part of the basement for my exercise room.
Even when we're apart, I think of you.

each other, one another—

Frankie and Johnny can't stand to be away from each other.
The three monkeys groomed one another's fur.

everybody—

Everybody in the room danced frantically.

every day, everyday—

It rains every day, every single day.
Fernando put on his everyday clothes.

every one, everyone—

Bruce ate every one of the cookies—every last one.
Everyone likes pizza.

in depth—

Study the biology textbook in depth.

in fact—

In fact, Janine wasn't in the room when the ruckus started.

in order—

In order to prove her point, Marty climbed onto the desk.

in spite of—

I like you in spite of your nasty disposition.

intact—

She's trying to keep her mind intact.

into, in to—

Ann Appleton fell into an easy job.
He came in to tell her how much he missed her.

in touch—

Please keep in touch with your sister.

itself—

The cat sunned itself.

myself—

I fixed the car myself.

nobody—

Nobody knows how Mr. Avengail makes his money.

no one —

No one ever calls me anymore.

nowadays —

Nowadays they call ice boxes "refrigerators."

nevertheless —

Nevertheless, Billy's in for a tough campaign.

some time —

I need some time alone.

sometimes —

Sometimes I get the blues.

somehow —

Somehow the laundry never gets done.

throughout —

Throughout the summer, David lounged on the beach.

whenever —

Whenever I hear that song, I start to cry.

whereas —

I'm always on time, whereas my brother is always late.

wherever —

Wherever Lillian goes, she goes in style.

withheld —

Joe withheld the rent because the roof leaked.

without—

You'll never catch Pearl without her sunglasses.

SPELLING

There's no getting around it—correct spelling takes patience. But you can save time by learning the rules. This is one of the more important ones.

I BEFORE E

Use I before E
Except after C
Or when sounded like A
As in neighbour and weigh.

bel*ie*ve	dec*ei*ve	fr*ei*ght
fr*ie*nd	rec*ei*ve	v*ei*n
p*ie*ce	conc*ei*t	

Exceptions—

w*ei*rd
for*ei*gn
l*ei*sure
s*ei*ze
th*ei*r

WORD ENDINGS: *S* AND *ED*

If word endings give you problems, train yourself to check every noun to see if it needs *s* and every verb to see if it needs *s* or *ed*. Remember that *s* on the end of a verb shows the verb is singular.

He jumps every time I ring the bell.
That horse makes consistently exceptional jumps.
Who keeps ringing the bell?

Add -ed—

• To form most simple past tenses.

She walked. He tripped. Mae asked a question.

- After *has, have, had.*

  He has walked. We have talked. She had already arrived.

- After the *be* verbs (*are, were, is, was, am, be, been, being*).

  They are prejudiced. She was depressed. He will be prepared.

Do not add -ed—

- After *to.*

  He loved to walk.

- After *would.*

  Every day he would walk five kilometres.

- After *did, didn't.*

  He didn't walk very often.

- After an irregular past tense.

  I bought bread.
  He found his keys.
  The cup fell.

Add -s—

- To form a plural of a noun (more than one).

  many scientists
  two potatoes

- To the present tense of a verb that follows *he, she, it,* or a singular noun.

  He walks.
  It talks.
  She says.
  The dog sees the hydrant.
  Bill asks.
  Polly insists.

Note: Usually when there is an *s* on the noun, there is no *s* on the verb.

Pots rattle.	A pot rattles.
The candles burn swiftly.	The candle burns swiftly.

• To form a possessive (with an apostrophe).

John's mother	today's society
Sally's house	women's clothing

Do not add -s—

• If there is an *s* on the subject of the sentence or if there are two subjects.

Tulips come from Holland.
Salt and sugar look the same.

• To the main verb, if one of these helping verbs comes before it.

does	may	will	must	would
shall	can	might	should	could

Kenneth cleans out the back seat of his car. *But ...*
Kenneth should clean out the back seat of his car.

Angelica gets there in thirty minutes. *But ...*
Angelica can get there in thirty minutes.

• When the word ends in -*y*.

When a verb ends in -*y* keep the *y* when you add -*ing*. To add -*s* or -*ed*, change the *y* to *i* or *ie*.

crying	cries	cried
studying	studies	studied
trying	tries	tried

When a noun ends in *y*, make it plural by changing the *y* to *i* and adding *es*.

activities	families	theories

But note—

Simply add *s* to nouns ending in *ey*.

journeys   monkeys   valleys

P or PP? T or TT?

Listen to the vowel before the added part. If the vowel sounds like its own letter name, *use only one consonant.*

writer   writing

If the vowel before the added part has a sound different from its name, *double the consonant.*

written

The same method works for *hoping* and *hopping*. Listen for the different sounds of the letter *o*. Here are some other examples.

beginning   dropping   quitting
stopped   occurred   referred

An exception: coming

WORDS WITH PREFIXES AND SUFFIXES

A prefix is added to the beginning of a word; a suffix is added to the end of a word. Both change the meaning or role of the word. When you add a prefix or suffix, you usually keep the spelling of the root word.

misspell   suddenness   dissatisfaction
hopeful   disappear   government
unnoticed   environment

The *-ly* endings also follow this rule.

really   totally   lonely   finally

An exception: true, truly

Other exceptions: The final *e* is usually dropped before a suffix that starts with a vowel.

debate, debatable   sense, sensible   love, lovable

Tricky Words

Look hard at the middle of each word.

definitely   probably
separate   interest
repetition   usually
opinion   necessary
embarrass   familiar
accommodate

AMERICAN VERSUS CANADIAN

Many words are spelled differently in Canada than they are south of the border. If you find yourself working for an American company or attending an American school, you'll want to use the American standard for spelling.

American	British, Canadian
analyze	analyse
canceled	cancelled
center	centre
check (all)	check (verify) cheque (bank draft)
color	colour
defense	defence
favorite	favourite
gray	grey
humor	humour
neighbor	neighbour
mold	mould
parlor	parlour
program	programme
smolder	smoulder
theater	theatre
traveled	travelled

TIPS FOR BECOMING A BETTER SPELLER

- Keep a list of your own problem words on the page provided at the end of this book.

- Write any word you misspell over and over until its spelling looks and feels natural.

- Sound out words. Use your hearing to help you spell words syllable by syllable.

- Make a habit of using your dictionary. If you have a strong vocabulary but trouble spelling, get yourself a spelling dictionary. A spelling dictionary doesn't include definitions and is faster to use if confirmation on spelling is all you're after.

- Borrow the eyes of others who are strong spellers, and have them help you improve your spelling.

- Learn the spelling rules. Know how prefixes and suffixes work. Memorize the exceptions.

CAPITALS

PROPER OR COMMON NOUNS

A word is capitalized when it is the specific name for a person, a place, or a thing. Common nouns aren't capitalized.

My grandmother is a sweetheart. *But* ...
He looked up when Grandmother Miller came into the room.

The myth spoke of an angry god. *But* ...
He prayed to God to give him strength.

He headed east along the TransCanada highway. *But* ...
He travelled to the Far East. *Also* ...
He was a member of the Eastern Orthodox church.

She's a university graduate. *But* ...
She went to Simon Fraser University.

They camped under the stars on the shore of the lake. *But* ...
They camped under the stars on the shore of Lake Superior.

DATES

The day and month are capitalized. So are holidays.

Tuesday, June, Remembrance Day

The seasons aren't capitalized.

Every spring, the roses bloom.

TITLES

People's titles are capitalized.

Dr. Maggie Dales
Professor Elliot O'Grady
L.T. Jerome, Jr.
Mark Smith, Ph.D.

In titles, the first word and all other major words are capitalized; *that, which, who,* and *whom* are capitalized. Articles (*a, an, the*), prepositions of four letters or less, and coordinating conjunctions (*and, or, but, so, ...*) are not capitalized.

"Dinner Along the Amazon"
"The Artist of the Beautiful"
"Ancestors' Graves in Kurakawa"
"Bartok and the Geranium"
"While I Was Looking at the Background You Walked from the Picture"

AFTER A COLON

If the words after the colon aren't a complete sentence, don't capitalize.

She had only one thought: getting a cup of coffee.

If the words after the colon are a complete sentence, you have a choice between beginning with a capital or leaving the first word lowercase. Just be consistent.

She had only one thought: She desperately wanted a cup of coffee.
She had only one thought: she desperately wanted a cup of coffee.

LISTS

When the listed items are in a complete sentence, capitalize. Use lowercase when they are not.

She made three resolutions this year: (1) She would get to bed before midnight each night. (2) She'd stop buying Smarties. (3) She wouldn't return his phone calls.

She made three resolutions this year: (1) early to bed, (2) no more Smarties, (3) no returning his calls.

QUOTATIONS

If the beginning of the sentence runs right into the quotation, don't capitalize.

She warned that "you better mean what you say" if you want to earn her respect.

If the beginning of the sentence is merely an introduction to the quotation, capitalize.

To earn her respect, she warned, "You better mean what you say."

COURSE NAMES

Capitalize school subjects when they are languages, or if you are naming a particular course. Otherwise, you don't need a capital.

psychology, Psychology 201, German

ABBREVIATIONS AND NUMBERS

ABBREVIATIONS

When in doubt, spell it out. You can abbreviate titles before and after a proper noun. You can also abbreviate the name of a well-known organization. You can abbreviate temperatures, dates, times, money, and numbers.

As a general rule, don't abbreviate—especially, don't use abbreviations like these in papers.

dept.	yr.	NY	Eng.	Thurs.
w/o	co.	&	gov't.	prof.

But do abbreviate words that you often see abbreviated, such as certain titles with proper names and well-known organizations.

- Titles before names.

    Mr. Mrs. Ms. Dr. Rev. St. Prof.

    Mr. Smith
    St. Joan of Arc

- Titles after names.

    Jr. Ph.D. M.D. M.A.

    Martin Luther King, Jr.
    Constance Beresford-Howe, Ph.D.

- Names of well-known organizations or countries.

CNIB	RCMP
CNR	TSN
CBC	U.S.A.
IBM	YMCA
LCBO	Xerox

• Abbreviate Dr. *only* before a name.

the doctor   Dr. Salk

Other Commonly Acknowledged Abbreviations

The following abbreviations are commonly used, if they accompany a number.

B.C.	(before Christ)	88 B.C.
A.D.	(after the year 0)	1954 A.D.
a.m.	(morning, before noon)	8 a.m.
p.m.	(after noon, and before midnight)	11 p.m.
No.	(number)	No. 12
$	(dollars)	$125

Note: Do not say—

That dinosaur was B.C.
The country changed A.D.
We left for the CNE early in the a.m.
He was supposed to come around in the p.m.
I had to look up her house No.
She owes me lots of $.

NUMBERS

If numbers are used infrequently, spell them out if one or two words long. If numbers are used frequently, use numerals for all numbers 11 or higher. Use numerals when referring to specific times, dates, addresses, identification numbers, chapters, pages, acts, scenes, fractions, decimals, percentages, statistics, and exact amounts of money.

Spell out—

• Numbers that take only one or two words.

nine   twenty-seven   two billion

- Numbers that begin a sentence.

    One hundred four years ago the ship sank.
    The ship sank 104 years ago.

- Numbers that form a compound word.

    a two-year-old baby

- Fractions.

    one-half

Use numerals for—

- Numbers that require three or more words.

    1,889   162

- Dates, page references, room numbers, statistics, addresses, percentages, and dollars and cents.

1889	7,500 residents	99.44%
page 2	221 B Baker Street	$5.98

- A list or series of numbers.

    1, 4, 9, 16, 25
    seats 12, 14, and 16

It is generally accepted that you can use numbers for the following.

ADDRESSES:	29 Yonge Street, Sudbury
FRACTIONS/DECIMALS:	5/8, 0.32
GAME RESULTS:	5–2, 6 to 3
PERCENTAGES:	99.7%, 10 percent
STATISTICS:	average grade 78 out of 100
DATES:	January 1, 1998
SURVEYS:	4 out of 10
PARTS OF PLAYS:	Act I, scene 1
IDENTIFICATION:	serial no. 334
DOLLAR AMOUNTS:	$83.47, $10
TIME:	6:00 a.m., 7:00 p.m.

Samples of Words Versus Numerals

I have eight cats.	I have 350 photos from my trip.
8:30 p.m.	June 30, 1995
3 Lundy's Lane	Serial No. 87-6315
Chapter 3, page 88	Act II, scene 3
3/4 cup	2.5 metres
99%	6:1
6 to 1	6–1
$88	No. 3

COMMAS (,)

You don't need a comma every time you breathe. Here are four places you need them.

- Put a comma before *and, but, so, yet, or, for,* and *nor* when they connect two sentences.

  The roads are slick, but you can make it.
  Gina intended to win the weight-lifting event, and that's exactly what she did.
  They called me in for a job interview, so I had to get new shoes.
  Not only did Melva run a restaurant, but she also wrote a cookbook.

However, don't automatically stick in a comma just because a sentence is long.

  The short man smoking a cigar and shouting at the hostess is my Uncle Jules.

- Use commas between parts of a list or series of three or more.

  I bought Perrier, Wheat Thins, and Velveeta for my party.
  Diamond climbed up the ladder, marched to the end of the diving board, took a big spring, and came down in a belly flop.

Also—

  In the class sat a bearded man, a police officer, a woman eating a sandwich, and a parakeet.

(Without the comma, what happens to the parakeet?)

Don't use a comma in a pair.

  I bought Perrier and Velveeta.
  Curt and Rixana are joining us this afternoon and going for a boat ride.
  Mary Ellen's mother handed out mints and made us sit while she played the piano.

- Use a comma after an introductory part of a sentence.

    However, Kathryn proved him wrong.
    For example, Larry built his own house.
    If we had left on time, we would be there by now.
    After we got home, she gave me a cup of that terrible herb tea.
    When James walked in, the whole family was laughing hysterically.

The comma separates the essential, independent part of the
sentence from the part that gives more information.

- Surround an insertion or interruption with a *pair* of commas.

    My cousin, who thinks she is always right, was dead wrong.
    Billy, of course, won the election.
    Scooby Doo, the Pekinese, has a cold.
    If you want to go with me, Sylvie, you'd better hurry up.
    Milton, even though no one invited him, arrived first at the party.

The above are wrong if you use only one comma. You need a
comma both at the beginning and at the end of the insertion or
interruption, to bracket it off from the rest. This insertion or
interruption isn't necessary to the sentence, but gives additional
information or adds interest.

Places and *dates* are treated as insertions. Note especially that
commas surround the year and the province.

    The hospital was in Kenora, Ontario, not far from the Manitoba
    border.
    I was born on August 15, 1954, at seven in the morning.

SEMICOLONS AND COLONS
(;) (:)

Semicolons can be used instead of periods; they also can separate parts of a complicated list. Colons create suspense: they set up a list, a quotation, or an emphatic statement and let the reader know that what's upcoming is important. Both signal a pause longer than that of a comma.

SEMICOLONS

- Use a semicolon to connect two related sentences; each half must be a complete sentence.

  He was fat; she was thin.
  Hope for the best; plan for the worst.
  I'll never forget the day of the circus; that's when I met the trapeze artist who changed my life.

A semicolon usually comes before certain transition words; a comma follows the transition. The following transition words shift the direction of the sentence and so require a longer pause— a more definite break—than a comma would allow.

however	therefore	otherwise
nevertheless	in other words	instead
for example	on the other hand	meanwhile
besides	furthermore	unfortunately

- A semicolon is preferable to a period when you want to emphasize a strong connection between the two sentences.

  Schubert was a great composer; however, Beethoven was greater.
  The bank lost two of my deposits; therefore, I am closing my account.

- Use semicolons instead of commas in a list when some of the parts already have commas.

To make it as an actor, you need, first of all, some natural talent; second, the habits of discipline and concentration; and third, the ability to promote yourself.

I've decided to wear shiny, outrageously high, black patent-leather shoes; a tomato red sequined dress, twenties style, knee length; and a soft, fluffy, feather boa, also red, wrapped twice around my neck.

If the writer of the above sentence used only commas, it would be too difficult to sort and separate the elements being described.

COLONS

Use a colon after a complete sentence to introduce related details. Before a colon you must have a *complete statement*. Don't use a colon after *are* or *include* or *such as*.

Colons can introduce—

- A list.

  I came home loaded with supplies: a tent, a sleeping bag, and a pack.

- A quotation.

  The author begins with a shocker: "Mother spent her summer sitting naked on a rock."

- An example.

  I love to eat legumes: for example, beans or lentils.

- An emphatic assertion.

  This is the bottom line: I refuse to work for only $5.50 an hour.

- Also, use a colon before a subtitle.

  Pablo Picasso: The Playful Artist

PERIODS, EXCLAMATION MARKS, AND QUESTION MARKS (.) (!) (?)

Each of these punctuation marks is used to note the end of a sentence. Each signifies the longest possible stop in a sentence.

A period is also used at the end of an abbreviation (Ms./Mrs./Mr.), but not between the letters in an acronym. Thus, YMCA, not Y.M.C.A., and IBM, not I.B.M.

An exclamation mark indicates surprise, an emphatic statement, or intense emotion. Use it sparingly.

A question mark indicates a direct question or an interrogative tone of voice.

> Miss Henrietta Bagg, the ancient woman who used to work at the YMCA's front desk, recently asked me to address her as Ms. Bagg. Imagine my surprise! Why does she, at eighty-eight, choose to change her title?

DASHES AND PARENTHESES (—) ( )

Dashes and parentheses separate a word or remark from the rest of the sentence.

Dashes

Dashes highlight the part of the sentence they separate, or show an abrupt change of thought in mid-sentence, or connect a fragment to a sentence.

> Buffy Sainte-Marie—born at Piapot Reserve, Saskatchewan, February 20, 1941—has gained a wide reputation as a socially conscious songwriter and performer.
> At night the forest is magical and fascinating—yet it terrifies me.
> Living the high life—that's what I want.

Dashes are very handy; they can replace a period, comma, colon, or semicolon. However, they are usually informal, so don't use many, or they will lose their effectiveness.

When you type, two hyphens make a dash. Do not space before or after the dash.

Parentheses

Parentheses de-emphasize the words they separate. Use them to enclose brief explanations or interruptions or afterthoughts. They can contain either part of a sentence or a whole sentence.

> I demanded a reasonable sum ($10.50 an hour), and they met my request.
> Polly's last movie disappointed both fans and critics. (See the attached reviews.)
> Marcia drives slowly (she claims her car won't go over 60 kilometres per hour), so she gets tickets for causing traffic jams.

Put any necessary punctuation *after* the second parenthesis if the parentheses contain part of a sentence.

If the parentheses contain a complete sentence, put the period *inside* the second parenthesis. Notice, however, that you don't capitalize or use a period when parentheses enclose a sentence within a sentence.

Be sparing with parentheses. Too many can chop up your sentences.

HYPHENS (-)

Hyphens join compound words.

self-employed
in-laws
seventy-five

Hyphens make a two-word adjective before a noun, but not after it.

Maggie has a high-paying job.
Maggie's job is high paying.

George Eliot was a nineteenth-century author.
George Eliot's prose is recognizably nineteenth century.

A hyphen can divide a multisyllable word at the end of a line. Divide only long words and only between syllables. When in doubt, do not divide.

Language evolves. Words not ordinarily associated are written separately. As an association forms, the word will become hyphenated. With time, the word may further evolve to read as one word.

years ago,	foot ball
once the game grew more popular,	foot-ball
now it's written as one word	football

In typing, use two hyphens to make a dash.

OTHER PUNCTUATION MARKS

BRACKETS [ ]

Square brackets are used to let the reader know that certain material wasn't mentioned in the original quote. You can add a pertinent editorial comment with a quotation, or make a statement within a statement.

> "She [Picquette] was older than I, but she had failed several grades ..." [Laurence, "The Loons" 339]

SLASHES   (/)

The slash separates two terms that apply equally (no space before or after). You can also use it to indicate line breaks when quoting poetry (space before and after).

> The friend/lover waited for her at the back of the hall.
> It's nice to have friends / to tell stories to

ELLIPSES   (...)

These three tightly spaced dots, with a space before and a space after, let your reader know that you have left out some portion of a quotation.

the original: "I won't go with you. You can't make me. You disgust me. I'm a free spirit. I'll do what I want."

using the ellipsis: "I won't go with you ... I'll do what I want."

APOSTROPHES (')

Apostrophes have two purposes: (1) they show ownership, and (2) they indicate a contraction. Most of the time, when you add an *s* to a word, you don't need an apostrophe. An apostrophe doesn't get added to show a plural noun.

Do not add an apostrophe; just add *s* or *es*—

* To make a plural.

    two bosses   three dogs   five shoes

* To a present-tense verb.

    He sees.   She says.   It talks.
    Rain falls.   Carol sings.

* To form plurals of numbers and abbreviations.

    1970s   VCRs

Add an apostrophe—

* To a contraction (put the apostrophe where the missing letter was).

    doesn't = does not   it's = it is   that's
    don't   I'm   weren't
    didn't   you're   what's

* To a possessive.

    John's hat   men's room   a night's sleep
    Ms. Jones's opinion   women's room   today's world
    Baldwin's sentences   people's feelings   babies' blankets

If the word is plural and already ends with *s*, just add an apostrophe after the *s*.

    my friends' apartment (several friends)

But note: Pronouns in possessive form have *no* apostrophe.

its   hers   his   ours   theirs   yours

- To the plural of a letter or a word out of context.

Sonia made all A's last fall
That last paragraph had five *really's* in it.

Note that the letter or word is italicized (or underlined).

QUOTATION MARKS (" ")

Use quotation marks any time you use someone else's exact words. If they are not the exact words, don't surround them with quotation marks.

Punctuation Before a Quotation

Here are three ways to lead into a quotation.

- For short quotations (a word or a phrase), don't say Alice Munro *says*, and don't put a comma before the quotation. Simply use the writer's phrase as it fits smoothly into your sentence.

  Alice Munro finds it "naïve" that people continue to ask her if the things in her stories really happened.

- Put a comma before the quotation marks if you use *he says/she says*. Put no comma if you use *he says/she says that*.

  Alice Munro says, "Yes, I use bits of what is real, in the sense of being really there and really happening, in the world, as most people see it, and I transform it into something that is really there and really happening, in my story" (in Geddes 827).

  Alice Munro says that she uses "bits of what is real ..."

- Use a colon (:) before a quotation of a sentence or more. Be sure you have a compete statement before the colon. Don't use *he says*.

  Alice Munro explains why she writes what she writes: "Who told me to write this story? Who feels any need of it before it is written? I do" (in Geddes 827).

Punctuation After a Quotation

At the end of a quotation, the period or comma goes *inside* the quotation marks. Do not close the quotation marks until the person's words end.

Munro supports the idea of using truth in fiction and writes: "The fictional room, town, world, needs a bit of starter dough from the real world."

Semicolons, Question Marks, and Exclamation Marks with Quotation Marks

Semicolons go outside closing quotation marks.

Munro says fiction "needs a bit of starter dough from the real world"; however, the people in her hometown of Wingham, Ontario, would no doubt prefer otherwise. (in Geddes 826)

Question marks and exclamation marks go inside if the person is asking or exclaiming. (If *you* as writer are asking or exclaiming, the mark goes outside.)

"Have you read 'Friend of My Youth'?" she asked.
Did Munro describe some of the questions she'd been asked as "naïve"?

When your quotation is more than a few words, let the quotation end your sentence. Otherwise you're liable to get a tangled sentence.

tangled: Munro says, "there is a difficulty about offending people in that town who would feel that use of this story is a deliberate exposure, taunt and insult" (in Geddes 826) illustrates her sensitivity to the issue of reality's place in fiction.

correct: Munro says, "there is a difficulty about offending people in that town who would feel that use of this story is a deliberate exposure, taunt and insult" (in Geddes 826). This quotation illustrates her sensitivity to the issue of reality's place in fiction.

INDENTING LONG QUOTATIONS

Long quotations (three or more lines) do not get quotation marks. Instead, start on a new line, then extra-indent the whole quotation in a block. After the quotation, return to the original margin and continue your paragraph.

Munro's character Del speaks of her and Naomi's curiosity about womanhood and sexuality:

> Naomi and I held almost daily discussions on the subject of sex, but took one tone, so that there were degrees of candour we could never reach. This tone was ribald, scornful, fanatically curious. A year ago we had liked to imagine ourselves victims of passion; now we were established as onlookers, or at most cold and gleeful experimenters. We had a book Naomi had found in her mother's old hope chest, under the moth-balled best blankets. (in Geddes 517)

Indicators to the Reader

An ellipsis means words are left out. Brackets mean you've added or changed a word to clarify the quotation's meaning.

> Sometimes the two girls, Del and Naomi, would pry and spy on family, the tenant, and her boyfriend. "Naomi was not popular in [Del's] house, nor [Del] in hers. Each ... was suspected ... in [Del's] case, of atheism, in Naomi's, of sexual preoccupation" (in Geddes 517).

DIALOGUE

In dialogue, start a new paragraph every time you switch from one speaker to another.

> "Did you enjoy reading 'Lives of Girls and Women'?" asked Professor Migliaccio.
> "I guess so," Joylene said, "but I was surprised by what some of the characters said and did."
> The professor thought a moment. "You know, I guess the story is so realistic as to have shock value. Munro is a little graphic in places."
> "Well, she sure shocked me," said Joylene. "I'd like to know why she wrote it that way."

Unless the quotation ends with a question mark or an exclamation point, use a comma to separate it from any explanatory words.

Writing About a Word or Phrase

When you discuss a word or phrase, surround it with quotation marks.

Advertisers use "new" and "free" as words to grab the consumer's attention.

The name "The Body Shop" is immediately associated with environmentally friendly skin and hair care products.

Do not use quotation marks around slang; either use the word without quotation marks or find a better word.

Quotation Within a Quotation

For quotations within a quotation, use single quotation marks.

According to radio announcer Rhingo Lake, "The jockey clearly screamed 'I've been foiled!' as the horse fell to the ground right before the finish line."

Quoting Poetry

When quoting two or more lines of poetry, extra-indent from the left margin and copy the lines exactly as the poet arranged them.

The following is taken from Colleen Still's poem for children, "Friends."

It's nice to have friends
to tell stories to,
to laugh with,
    sing with,
    jump with,
    dream with,
    cry with,
    play with,
    explore with,
    stay with.
It's nice to have friends,
isn't it?

When quoting *a few* words of poetry that include a line break, use a slash mark to show where the poet's line ends.

In *The Tempest*, Shakespeare calls us "such stuff / As dreams are made on."

UNDERLINING OR QUOTING TITLES

Underline or italicize titles of longer works: books, magazines, newspapers, plays. Use quotation marks for titles of shorter works or for parts of longer works.

Canadian Living
The Globe and Mail
Exotica
Who Has Seen the Wind?
The Mousetrap

"Little Miss Muffet"
"Life is a Highway"
"Heart of Gold"
"The Monkey's Paw"
"Lives of Girls and Women"

Anne of Green Gables (the book)
"Anne of Green Gables" (the TV show)

Note: Do not underline or place quotation marks around your title on a cover sheet—unless your title contains someone else's title.

My Week on a Shrimp Boat
An Analysis of Atwood's Short Story "Hairball"
Man Against Man in Timothy Findley's *The Wars*.

PART FIVE
OTHER THINGS THAT ARE GOOD TO KNOW

- *Introduction*
- *Proofreader's/Editor's Symbols*
- *Proofreader's Checklist*
- *Most Frequent Errors at a Glance and How to Avoid Them*
- *Evaluation Form for Any Piece of Writing*
- *Memo*
- *Letter*
- *Summary*
- *Research Essay on Literature*
- *Commonly Misspelled Words*
- *Not a Word*
- *Personal Speller*
- *Vocabulary List*
- *Irregular Verbs*
- *Your Rules of Thumb*
- *One Day, Some Day*
- *Postscript*

INTRODUCTION

If you have spent some time with Parts One to Four, you should now feel more comfortable with the process of researching, planning your writing, writing, making decisions on format, proofreading, and editing your work. If you have taken in and understood the concepts in the previous four parts, you may now need only a fleeting reminder about suggested rules for writing.

Part Five can be thought of as a book within a book — as a self-contained mini-handbook. It offers practical tools to help you evaluate and improve your own work. It briefly reviews the most common problems found in a piece of writing and shows you some solutions to those problems.

Part Five also includes writing samples that you can use as a guide when writing a memo, letter, summary, or research paper. There is also space for you to jot down your own useful thoughts on the writing process and ideas for future pieces of writing.

What follows is a summary of the entire book. We hope and expect these final pages will be highlighted and dog-eared, as a sign of their repeated usefulness.

PROOFREADER'S/EDITOR'S SYMBOLS

If a teacher, employer, or editor has gone over your work and wants you to make some adjustments, the following are some of the more common abbreviated symbols indicating where a change is recommended.

abbr	abbreviation difficulty
adj	misuse of adjective
adv	misuse of adverb
awk	awkward
cap	capital letter
case	error in case
cit	missing citation, documentation problem
cl	cliché
◡	close up space
co	coherence is lacking
cs	comma splice
℘	delete
det	need more details, examples, specifics
dm	dangling modifier
format	error in format
frag	sentence fragment
jar	jargon
lc	need lowercase
??	meaning unclear
mixed	mixed construction
mm	misplaced modifier
mood	error in mood
∧	omission, add word, insert something
¶	need to start new paragraph
p	punctuation error
∧̣	add comma
∧̣	add semicolon
⊙	add colon
∨̈∨̈	add quotation marks
⊙	add period
pro agr	pronoun antecedent error (singular and plural mixed)

rep.	repetitious
shift	shift in tone, mood, tense
#	separate with a space
sl	slang
sp	spelling
sex.	sexist language used
ss	sentence structure
t	error in verb tense
⒯ⓡ	transpose letters or words
ungr.	ungrammatical
vague	vague, unclear reference
var	need more variety
vb	error in verb form or verb agreement
w	wordy
wc	diction, word choice
//	faulty parallel
X	something isn't working

PROOFREADER'S CHECKLIST

The most frequent types of errors are listed below. Keep this list handy when proofreading any piece of writing.

1. Design of content
2. Sentence fragments
3. Comma splices and run-ons
4. Subject/verb agreement
5. Passive voice
6. Shift in tense
7. Shift in point of view
8. Pronoun antecedent agreement
9. Pronoun case
10. Vague reference
11. Dangling modifier
12. Misplaced modifier
13. Faulty parallelism
14. Parts of speech
15. Word choice
16. Sentence variety
17. Repetitious writing
18. Conjunctions, subordination, sentence structure, word placement
19. Mixed construction
20. Articles
21. Spelling
22. Punctuation

Following is an explanation of the specific problems and some possible solutions to them.

MOST FREQUENT ERRORS AT A GLANCE AND HOW TO AVOID THEM

1. Design of Content

Do you have a meaningful, specific, supportable thesis? Are your arguments well developed and well supported? Is your essay balanced? That is, are your points in body paragraphs one, two, and three equal in weight, importance, and quantity and quality of evidence? Do you have an interesting opening, a meaty and sensible middle, and a logical and memorable ending?

2. Sentence Fragments

problems:

> After I went to the store.
> Really.
> Sitting patiently by the window, waiting for my brother, wondering what could be holding him up.
> Because I've run out of money.

The above have been punctuated like sentences, which they are not. To fix a sentence fragment, try these: get rid of the dependent clause cue; join the dependent clause to an independent clause; add the missing subject and verb; put a comma between the fragment and the thought it's attempting to complete or explain.

solutions:

> I went to the store.
> After I went to the store, I had to go back to the bank.
> Do you really believe that?
> Sitting patiently by the window, waiting for my brother, wondering what could be holding him up, I decided to call our parents' home.
> I hope you can pick up the tab, because I've run out of money.

3. Comma Splices and Run-ons

problem:

> You must be joking I can't believe you ate the whole banana split on your own, I thought you were going to save me at least a bite unbelievable.

In a run-on sentence, the writer has come to the end of a complete thought but has failed to put in a "full stop" punctuation mark.

The easiest way to correct a run-on is to put in a period if the next sentence isn't closely related to the first, or a semicolon if there is a close relationship between the two parts. Another solution is to use joiner words to connect the separate ideas; still another is to play around with language and knock out some words, to make one part dependent on the main sentence. The independent clause has the power to drive the sentence forward. The dependent clause does not; it needs to be pulled along by the main and complete thought.

solution:

> You must be joking. I can't believe you ate the whole banana split on your own; I thought you were going to save me at least a bite. You're unbelievable. *or* ...
> You must be joking. I can't believe you ate the whole banana split on your own, instead of saving me at least a bite. You're unbelievable.

4. Subject/Verb Agreement

In the problems that follow, the verb doesn't match the subject in number: a singular subject is inappropriately matched with a plural verb, or a plural subject is inappropriately matched with a singular verb.

problems:

> The Smith family are moving in next door.
> Charlotte and Emily, who are very close friends with my sister, lives next door to my boyfriend.
> The children plays in the schoolyard after school.

Economics are a hard course of study.
Ten kilometres are a lot to walk in a day.
Either Jen or the twins is coming to baby-sit for me on the weekend.
Either the twins or Jen are coming to baby-sit for me on the weekend.

The verb must match the subject of the sentence in number. If the subject is more than one, the verb must be plural; if the subject is only one, the verb must be singular. Some situations are trickier than others. Remember that collective nouns (family, team, jury, class, audience) usually take a *singular* verb unless the emphasis is on the individual actions of the members of the group. Weight, size, and distance require a singular verb. Some nouns (economics, aerobics), despite the *s* on the end, are regarded as one thing and so require a singular verb. If the word "or" separates the elements of the subject, the verb should match in number with the last noun named. Be sure you can identify the subject of the sentence, and remember that the subject of the sentence is never found in a prepositional phrase.

solutions:

The Smith family (one unit) is (singular) moving in next door.
Charlotte and Emily (they), who are very close friends with my sister (dispensable), live (plural) next door to my boyfriend.
The children (plural) play (plural) in the schoolyard after school.
Economics (one subject) is (singular) a hard course of study.
Ten kilometres (one length of distance) is (singular) a lot to walk in a day.
Either Jen or the twins (plural, and the noun after "or" that is closest to the verb) are (plural, matching "twins") coming to baby-sit for me this weekend.
Either the twins or Jen (singular, and the noun after "or" that is closest to the verb) is (singular, matching "Jen") coming to baby-sit for me this weekend.

5. Passive Voice

In the following, *is* and *are* operate as passive verbs. When a sentence contains a passive verb, you can't necessarily tell who or what is performing the action. The result can be an unclear or confusing sentence, and one that lacks energy.

problems:

> Money is made an issue and the bills are unpaid again.
> The kite is flown.
> The last cookie is gone.

To fix these, name the significant participants in the action. Then substitute active verbs for the passive verbs.

solutions:

> Money remains a big issue for the couple, since the bills are unpaid again. *or ...*
> His wife brings up the issue of money when she sees he hasn't paid the bills again. *or ...*
> They have an issue with money, and can't ever seem to pay their bills on time. *or ...*
> When he sees the unpaid bills, he raises the issue of money with his wife.

> The kite is flown by Mark. *or ...*
> Mark flew the kite.

> I ate the last cookie.

6. Shift in Tense

In the following, the time of the action changes for no apparent reason. Sometimes this shift in logical: I went to Mexico last winter, and will go there again next year. Often, it isn't.

problems:

> I went to the store and buy bananas.
> It was a good party. You should come too.

Decide whether the action took place in the past, is taking place in the present, or will take place in the future. Be consistent unless there is a logical reason for going back and forth in time.

solutions:

> I went to the store and bought bananas. (past)
> I go to the store and buy bananas. (present)

It was a good party. You should have come too. (past)
It's a good party. Come on over. (present)

7. Shift in Point of View

In the following, the writer has started out using pronouns in the first person, but then shifted to another person. Sometimes this makes sense: We went to the park and he fell off the swing. Often, it doesn't.

problems:

I like to ride my bike, because it's good for your legs.
We must proofread our work very carefully, because if we don't, you'll see what you were intending to write rather than what made it to the page.

Don't shift the pronoun choice, unless the meaning of the sentence requires it.

solutions:

I (1st person singular) like to ride my (1st person singular) bike, because it's good for my (1st person singular) legs.
We (1st person plural) must proofread our (1st person plural) work very carefully, because if we (1st person plural) don't, we'll (1st person plural) see what we (1st person plural) were intending to write rather than what made it to the page.

8. Pronoun Antecedent Agreement

In the following, a pronoun doesn't agree in number with the word to which it refers.

problems:

Everyone must wash their hands before dinner.
Tom, Ted, and Tony got into his costume.

If the first noun or pronoun is singular, what follows and refers back to it must also be singular. If the first noun or pronoun is plural, what follows and refers back to it must also be plural.

Watch out for *anyone, anybody, anything, everyone, everybody, everything, someone, somebody, something.* These are all singular, and require singular pronouns for agreement.

solutions:

> Everyone (singular) must wash his/her hands (singular) before dinner. *or …*
> They (plural) must wash their (plural) hands before dinner. *or …*
> People (plural) must wash their (plural) hands before dinner.
>
> Tom (singular) got into his costume (singular). *or …*
> Tom, Ted, and Tony (they—plural) got into their (plural) costumes.

9. Pronoun Case

Pronouns can perform different functions in a sentence. An object pronoun cannot be the subject of a sentence; a subject pronoun cannot be the object.

problems:

> Whom called yesterday?
> Mac and me went to the barn.
> Give it to she.
> Who should I address the letter to?
> Hand me hat to me.

I, you, he, she, it, who, we, and *they* function as subjects. *Me, you, him, her, it, whom, us,* and *them* function as objects. *My, your, his, her, whose, its, our,* and *their* are possessive pronouns.

solutions:

> Who (subject) called yesterday?
> Mac and I (subject) went to the barn.
> Give it to her (object).
> To whom (object) should I address the letter?
> Hand my (possessive) hat to me.

10. Vague Reference

Pronouns can be used to substitute for nouns. A problem arises if the reader can't easily tell which noun is being substituted.

problem:

> I told them so many times, don't leave the door open, check that the stove is off, clean your room, and I come home today to find he hadn't done it.

To avoid confusion, be sure—if there is any question—that you rename the person, place, or thing.

solution:

> I told my two sons so many times, don't leave the door open, check that the stove is off, clean your room, and I come home today to find Ted, the eldest, hadn't even locked the door.

11. Dangling Modifier

A modifier is a word or grouping of words that gives more information or description about someone or something in the sentence. Sometimes the modifier is describing something that isn't named in the sentence.

problems:

> Studying hard all semester, his parents were still disappointed with his grades.
> Opening the door for the woman behind him, the dog bit her leg.
> After she graduated from college, the baby was put into daycare.

Be sure the person or thing being described is clearly named. A reader shouldn't have to wonder what is going on. It should be easy to tell who's who and what's what. There should be a clear relationship between the description and what is being described.

solutions:

> Even though he studied hard all semester, his parents were still disappointed with his grades.

The dog bit the woman's leg as its owner opened the door for her.
After she graduated from college, the young mother put her baby
into daycare.

12. Misplaced Modifier

Sometimes the arrangement of elements in a sentence creates a
different picture in the reader's mind than the writer intended.
These images can be funny—or embarrassing. Remember that a
reader will think the modifier is describing the person, place, or
thing it's nearest to in the sentence.

problems:

She served hot dogs to the children on the barbecue.
She ate the ice cream on the park bench.

Move the modifier to beside what's being described.

solutions:

She served barbecued hot dogs to the children.
While sitting on the park bench, she ate the ice cream.

13. Faulty Parallelism

If the parts of a sentence perform the same function and have the
same importance, they need to have the same grammatical form.
The following sentences don't follow this principle.

problems:

Three things contributing to the strength of this book are that its plot
is full of suspenseful conflict, its characters are complicated and full of
surprises, and well-written dialogue.
Lots of students find it frustrating to study and read questions on an
exam.
She decided to buy a nice red dress, a tasteful tapestry purse, and
choosing a pair of off-white sling-backs.
George likes cross-country skiing, downhill skiing, and to dive.

Rephrase those elements which are coordinated in a list so that
they are similar in terms of meaning, form, and part of speech.

solutions:

> Three things contributing to the strength of this book are the plot, which is full of suspense, the characters, who are complicated and full of surprises, and the dialogue, which is true to life and well written.
> Lots of students find it frustrating to study for and read questions on an exam.
> She decided to buy a nice red dress, a tasteful tapestry purse, and a pair of off-white sling-backs.
> George likes cross-country skiing, downhill skiing, and high diving.

14. Parts of Speech

Different forms of words perform different functions in a sentence. A writer will occasionally choose an adjective when an adverb is required, or vice versa, or a noun when a verb is required, or vice versa.

problems:

> You dance bad.
> I feel badly.
> I complaint to the doctor.
> I have a complaining for you.

Be sure you have the correct form for the function you are requiring of the selected word.

> e.g., beauty – noun
>   beautify – verb
>   beautiful – adjective
>   beauteous – adjective
>   beautifully – adverb

solutions:

> You dance badly. (adverb describing verb *dance*)
> I feel bad. (With linking verbs, like *am,* or state-of-being verbs, like *feel,* the modifier describes the subject, not the verb and so needs to be an adjective, not an adverb.)
> I complained (verb in past tense) to the doctor.
> I have a complaint (noun) for you.

The dictionary notes the part of speech after every word listed.

n. = noun (person, place, or thing)
v. = verb (action word, or state-of-being word)
v.t. = verb used transitively (requires a direct object, e.g., *They raised 50 dollars.*)
v.i. = verb used intransitively (doesn't need a direct object e.g., *He laughed.*)
pron. = pronoun (a word that substitutes for a noun)
adj. = adjective (a word that modifies a noun or pronoun)
adv. = adverb (a word that modifies a verb, adjective, or other adverb)
prep. = preposition (a word preceding a noun or pronoun that gives information about the noun's position, placement, direction, time, relationship)
conj. = conjunction (a word that links and relates part of a sentence)
interj. = interjection (a word that can stand on its own or be inserted to command attention)

15. Word Choice

A sloppy writer all too often resorts to a boring phrase, a nonexistent word, too vague a word, sexist language, colloquialisms or slang, clichés, overly technical diction, or pretentious words.

problems:

It was a hot day.
They faced the mirror and watched themself dancing.
Society said to leave your shoes at the door.
He stood before a female judge.
Like, be like Margaret Atwood and go crazy with words.
Time stood still, her pulse raced, as she looked into his face.
He studied the comet's trajectory with unabridged focus.
This wine is slightly presumptuous, but eminently palatable.
Irregardless of the time, I'm staying up to see the end of this movie.
Anyways, you can go on to bed if you want.

Put yourself in the reader's shoes. Imagine how an objective reader might view your choice of words. Use vivid, concrete, correct, specific, nonsexist, appropriate, fresh, meaningful, simple, and direct language.

solutions:

> With the intense sun beating down on her, she found the day an unbearable scorcher.
> They faced the mirror and watched themselves (correct word) dancing.
> The company's board of directors (more specific) said to leave your shoes at the door.
> He stood before a judge. (Don't mention female, if you wouldn't mention male; otherwise a reader will conceivably find your sentence sexist.)
> Be like Margaret Atwood and have fun with language. (no Valley Girl sound here)
> Looking into his face, she felt excited, and lost all sense of time. (not so much of a cliché)
> He studied the comet's path with care. (more easily understood)
> The wine is acceptable. (simplified)
> Regardless (a real word) of the time, I'm staying up to see the end of the movie.
> (nonstandard word eliminated) You can go on to bed if you want.

16. Sentence Variety

Sentences can feel cumbersome, plodding, or choppy if they're too similar in structure.

problems:

> I took the train. I ate at the station. I lost my wallet. I found it an hour later.
> She's tall. My sister is tall too. My brother is tall also.
> A few drops of rain fell at the parade. A few floats went by. A few people left.

Try varying the language and the sentence types.

solutions:

> I took the train. After I'd arrived, while eating at the station, I lost my wallet. It was a scary hour before my wallet turned up.

She's tall, but I'm used to that. Both my sister and my brother are tall, too.
A few drops of rain fell at the parade. Only a couple of floats went by before some of the people left.

Listed below are the possible sentence types.

simple: The dog ran. (has no subordinating clauses)
complex: Don't take one bite of that until you take off your hat. (one independent clause, and one or more subordinate clauses)
compound: The dog ran quickly, but the cat could run even faster. (two independent clauses, usually joined with a comma and a coordinating conjunction)
compound-complex: Show me your favourite restaurant, and I'll take you to mine, where I met my second husband. (two independent clauses and at least one subordinate clause)

17. Repetitious Writing

Sometimes words or sentences feel too familiar, or monotonous, or empty of meaning.

problems:

> I very much like to go to the movies. I really like sitting in the dark-ened theatre, and really get into it, as the first images come up on the screen.
> He gave my son such a big, huge, large ball for his birthday.

Edit out any words or phrases that are repetitious and that don't add emphasis or stylistic flavour.

solutions:

> I like going to the movies. When I sit in the darkened theatre, I get right into it as the first images come up on the screen.
> He gave my son such a big ball for his birthday.

18. Conjunctions, Subordination, Sentence Structure, Word Placement

Sometimes two parts of a sentence are treated as balanced when one portion should clearly be more important. Sometimes the placement of words, phrases, or clauses is unnatural and cumbersome.

problems:

> He came in late again from work, she decided to leave her husband.
> She bought a new dress, her father died last week.
> Going back in time for me really can cause pain too great.
> Unbelievable, thought he, when looking in his bank book, realized it was empty.

Decide which portion of your sentence has the main idea; then rephrase the rest so that it isn't competing for attention with the central thrust of the sentence. Read your work aloud so that you can hear which pattern or arrangement of parts is smoothest and most meaningful.

solutions:

> She decided to leave her husband, since she knew all too well why he came in late again from work.
> Her father died last week, so she went out to buy a black dress for the funeral.
> For me, going back in time can cause too much pain.
> Unbelievable, he thought, as he looked in his bank book and realized his account was empty.

19. Mixed Construction

Sometimes the second part of a sentence doesn't naturally flow from the first. The writer has begun the piece in one direction, then changed structure in a way that doesn't make sense. Sometimes writers mix metaphors or make comparisons in the same sentence of things that really don't belong together. Or they use the word "where" instead of "when" to describe an activity.

problems:

> With spring coming and the rain pouring down, put fertilizer on the grass.
> It's six to one and a bird in the hand.
> Although Carlos knows many languages, but he still has trouble coming up with some words in English.
> Because Maria is a talented dancer, consequently she should consider joining the Toronto Premiere Dance Theatre.
> Jealousy is where someone else has something you want.
> Every bit as beautiful are the Canadian Badlands in Alberta to the American Badlands in the Dakotas.

Ensure that the second half of the sentence naturally flows from the first.

solutions:

> With spring coming and the rain pouring down, it makes sense to get out there and put fertilizer on the grass.
> It's six of one, half a dozen of the other.
> Although Carlos knows many languages, he still has trouble coming up with some words in English.
> Maria is a talented dancer; she should consider joining the Toronto Premiere Dance Theatre.
> One is jealous when one wants what someone else has.
> The Canadian Badlands in Alberta are every bit as beautiful as the American Badlands in the Dakotas.

20. Articles

Particularly for people for whom English is a second language, knowing which article to use when can be a problem.

problems:

> Jeff goes to bar and plays Friday night.
> Jeff goes to bar and gets drunk Friday night.
> Give me telephone.
> He ran to neighbours to get ice for my cut.

solutions:

> Jeff goes to the (a particular) bar and plays each Friday night.
> Jeff goes to a (any) bar and gets drunk every Friday night.
> Give me the (specific) telephone.
> Give me a (any) telephone for my birthday.
> He ran to the (specific) neighbours to get ice for my cut.
> He ran to a neighbour's house to get ice for my cut. (not a particular neighbour)

21. Spelling

Some words are more commonly misspelled than others. The most common mistakes are these: missed apostrophes, apostrophes where they aren't required, no *s* on plural nouns, no *s* on singular verbs in the third person, *i* before *e* after *c*, and incorrect choice of sound-alikes.

problems:

> Its up to you.
> She gave the dog it's bone.
> There were so many cookie from which to chose, he had trouble picking just won.
> I recieve your meaning.
> He decided he wanted to come to.
> Their always late. Alot of people hate that.
> The women who is always at the cash desk only wears black.

Know the words you regularly misspell. Watch for these trouble spots in any piece of work you generate. When using a computer, use spellcheck, but realize it won't catch some of the errors. Borrow someone else's eyes. Return to your work later and take a fresh look at what you've written. Keep a personal speller of words that cause you difficulty. When in doubt, check the dictionary.

solutions:

> It's up to you.
> She gave the dog its bone.
> There were so many cookies from which to choose, he had trouble picking just one.
> I receive your meaning.

He decided he wanted to come, too.
They're always late. A lot of people hate that.
The woman who is always at the cash desk only wears black.

22. Punctuation

Many writers overuse and underuse different punctuation marks. While there are recommended rules, many writers use punctuation in a characteristic way that shows an individual style. Know the rules, and if you break them, know why a deviation from the usual standard is advisable or acceptable.

,   Short pause.
     Don't use before items in a list or series.
     problem: He brought, wine, cheese, and a candle.
     Don't use with restrictive elements.
     problem: The boy, who has green hair, stole my drink.
     Don't use between subject and verb.
     problem: My neighbours in the big house next door, have more money than they know what to do with.
;   Slightly longer pause. Used to separate elements in a list that already have internal punctuation, or between two independent but related clauses. Don't use to introduce a significant point.
     problem: That period in her life taught her two important things; to listen closely and to reserve judgment.
:   Slightly longer pause. Calls attention to what comes after, or separates intros from quotations, and parts from wholes.
( ) For an afterthought, separate thought, or minor digression.
[ ] For an insertion in an otherwise word-for-word quotation.
—   Separates thought that deserves special emphasis.
... For words deleted in an otherwise word-for-word quotation.
-    For compound words (*sister-in-law*).
/   For poetry lines running together, or separation of options (*pass/fail*).
.   Long, full stop.
!   Expresses surprise or emotion at end of thought.
?   To indicate a question.
" " For titles of short pieces, direct quotations, or dialogue.
' ' For a quote within a quotation.
'   For a contraction (*it's*), or ownership (*Ben's, James' or James's*).

EVALUATION FORM FOR ANY PIECE OF WRITING

When you are rereading your work, make sure you consider the following. Your piece of writing will fall somewhere between weak and strong.

Teachers, employers, and editors will also find this form useful.

	Severe difficulties	Needs work	OK	Good	Very good	Getting there	Yes! You're there
TITLE							
SHAPE Structure/arrangement of parts. Intro/grabber/hook. Focus/angle/thesis/point. Balanced middle/body. Punchy, memorable, appropriate conclusion. Paragraphs.							
CONTENT							
Centred, focused. Logical sequence of ideas. Well developed, strong use of details, examples. Thoughtful, significant, memorable, interesting. Specific, clear language. Well chosen, concrete, vivid words. Avoids - slang - sexist language - overly technical language - pretentious language Effectively fulfils the purpose.							

	Severe difficulties	Needs work	OK	Good	Very good	Getting there	Yes! You're there
CONTENT							
Original sense of style. Writer's involvement evident. Affects the reader.							
MECHANICS/CRAFTING							
Spelling - i before e - sound-alikes - other Punctuation , ; : . - other Frags Run-ons Comma splices Agreement - pronoun - subj/vb Conjunctions Subordination No shifts - point of view - tense - parallelism Modifiers - dangling - misplaced Format Documentation - parenthetical references - works cited							
OVERALL COMMENTS:							

WEAKNESSES
THINGS TO AVOID IN
  FUTURE
STRENGTHS
THINGS TO KEEP DOING
  IN FUTURE							

MEMO

A memorandum is a piece of communication distributed within an institution or corporation. It is used most often to announce an employee's coming or going or a new procedure, or to share or request information.

When writing a memo, anticipate any questions the readers may have. Remember to answer *who, what, where, when, why,* and *how.* Be sure to specify what action, if any, you would like the reader to take.

There is a certain etiquette to follow in terms of format. Put the receiver's name before your own name. Alphabetize the names if the memo is going to more than one person. Be sure to note the day, month, and year. Give the memo a subject title so that it can be easily retrieved should there be a future need.

M E M O R A N D U M

TO: Shelley Brown   Charles Simmons
        Tim Coates   Chris Timmons
        Deborah Milne   Robert Tyler
        Candace Martin   John Wong

FROM: Sandra Maracle

DATE: September 21, 1995

SUBJECT: Voicemail Procedure

A communications consultant has been analyzing our present use of our voicemail system and has some suggestions for improvement. Ms. Nancy Whittaker has agreed to conduct a training session for each department head. Please RSVP and send any of your specific voicemail training requests to me at my E-mail address (smara) or via voicemail (ext 3531).

Please arrange for another department representative, should you be unable to attend.

DATE: Thursday, September 28, 1995
TIME: 11:00 a.m. to noon
PLACE: Vice President's Boardroom, 5th Floor, Rm. 508

LETTER

A letter is a piece of correspondence that is sent outside an institution or corporation. Its purpose could be to complain, inform, educate, request, or persuade. Every effort is made to anticipate and answer the reader's questions.

If the letter isn't written on letterhead, the return address should be clearly noted in the upper right-hand corner. The date follows, flush left. Then put the receiver's name, title, and complete address, also flush left. The body of the letter begins with *Dear* and the receiver's name, followed by a comma if the receiver is a friend, or a colon if the letter is more formal.

The first paragraph grabs the reader's attention and states what the letter is about. The middle paragraphs flesh out the topic introduced in the first paragraph. The closing paragraph lets the reader know what action is requested.

The closing is followed by a comma. Space is left for a signature. The sender's name is typed flush left under the closing. The next line is reserved for the sender's position or title. Two spaces down, the initials in caps note the sender, and the initials in lowercase note the typist. A "c.c." at the bottom of the page followed by a name lets the reader know who else received a copy of the letter. The notation "/encl." tells the reader that something is accompanying the letter.

R.R. #1
Woodlawn, Ontario
K0A 3M0

September 8, 1995

Mr. Peter Gzowski
"Morningside"
CBC Radio
P.O. Box 500, Station A
Toronto, Ontario
M5W 1E6

Dear Mr. Gzowski:

I am a devoted listener to "Morningside." I have lived in Vancouver and Nelson in B.C., Edmonton and Red Deer in Alberta, Brandon in Manitoba, Kenora, and now outside Ottawa. Happily, in each location, I've been able to listen to your insights and the insights and experiences of your well-chosen interviewees. Your researchers seem to have a knack for discovering interesting people and events all across this great land of ours.

I now find myself living next door to a most remarkable woman. She has been blind since childhood yet paints the most brilliant and intriguing paintings in acrylics. I've shared many pots of tea with Edith and never tire of hearing her philosophy of life and art. She sees colour and shape in her mind's eye, although her eyesight forbids her that gift. I believe she would make an intriguing guest for your show.

I have enclosed some of my humble efforts at photographing some of her artwork. I trust you can see the power of her images.

Should you be interested in having a radio conversation with Edith, have one of your researchers call me at 613-555-9066. Edith lives without a phone, but I'll see she gets back in touch with you. I will be in the city early in November and would gladly bring Edith to your studio, at a time appropriate for taping.

I trust her story is one that your other devoted listeners would want to hear.

Sincerely,

[signed]
Margaret Smith

MS
/encl.

SUMMARY

You write a summary if you are asked to condense an article, story, or novel and highlight its contents. Often the writer gives a summary before reviewing or evaluating an event or other piece of writing. A strong summary accurately represents events, atmosphere, tone, and intention. It retells the main plot points or story line in brief. A summary condenses the original piece of writing, capturing its essence and highlights.

Atwood's *The Robber Bride* in Brief

Though a hefty 545 pages in hardcover, *The Robber Bride* is a fast read. In a sense, it is three compelling books in one. *The Robber Bride* is a book of histories—the three distinct histories three interesting women endure with a common enemy, Zenia.

The adventure begins in The Toxique, a trendy restaurant on Queen West in Toronto. Tony, Roz, and Charis, an unlikely but long-established trio, are gathered for a pleasantly distracting lunch when each in turn is horrified at Zenia's return from the dead four-and-a-half years after they've buried her.

Tony, a diminutive history scholar and eccentric university professor, hides in her basement replaying battles of old, rearranging words backwards, and speculating on the meaning of her archrival's re-entry into the land of the living. Tony knows Zenia is up to no good and is more than a little afraid she'll once more stick her sharp nails into Tony's cherished musicologist husband, West.

Charis, Toronto Islander and herb-growing, crystal-gazing innocent, quakes at the sight of Zenia. The exotic woman's reappearance brings back a flood of memories of Charis's kindnesses to Zenia—and Zenia's many betrayals. Zenia lies. Zenia uses. Zenia cheats. Zenia steals other women's men. She did the unspeakable with and to Charis's only love, Billy, now long disappeared, many thanks to Zenia.

Roz tries to appear cool, but her old rage at Zenia returns. Roz quickly uses some of her great gobs of money to have her faithful detective follow the phantom. Roz wanders through her oversized house, wrestling with fashion and jewellery decisions and trying to ground herself somehow in the chaos generated by her three children, all the while waiting for her sleuth's diagnosis of this unthinkable situation. Zenia many years earlier had pulled Roz's distinguished Mitch from their comfortable and long-established love nest; she was the catalyst for his demise and death.

The three can't forget. They can't forgive. They can't trust Zenia. Instead, Tony, Charis, and Roz each silently, independently, reflect on the devastation Zenia brought to their lives. Each hides away, pained by memories and terrified of the inevitable horrors ahead. The university friends gather, confer, conspire, and analyze. What is Zenia up to? What does she want? What's left of theirs for her to rob? And Zenia, still so exceptionally beautiful, strides in, cool and confident like a fashion model, dense cloud of dark tendrilled hair blowing, to slam a sharpened, vengeful stiletto heel through each of their three expectant hearts.

Zenia takes, greedily, outrageously, and without morality. But with her unexpected reappearance, she also gives these three women a heightened self-awareness—new drama, energy, and life.

RESEARCH ESSAY ON LITERATURE

When writing a research essay on literature, there are some points to keep in mind.

- The paper is not merely biographical info about the author's life.

- The paper is not merely a summary of the poem, story, novel, or play.

- You must have a point to make.

- The underlying thesis should be specific enough to reflect your original take on the topic, but not so narrow as to make finding support overly difficult.

- The essay is your point of view first and foremost; paraphrases and quotations are there as back-up, to provide additional proof.

- You can employ logic, emotion, and/or charisma.

- You must know your audience and purpose. In some cases the professor, employer, or publisher will want you to avoid the first-person pronoun "I."

- Design the shape of the essay and build your case.

- Grab interest. Announce or suggest what you will be proving, then prove it, and then summarize your writing in a memorable way.

- Review your essay as if seeing it for the first time. Make sure you have accomplished your purpose.

APPEALING TO THE URGE TO LOOK AND SEE:
HOW WRITERS GET READERS TO INVEST IN A GLIMPSE

Professor's Name, EN170   Student's Name
November 8, 1995   Student Number

It's getting colder. With windows and doors shutting, so closes any ready access to those easy glimpses into other lives. Canadians will soon be collecting stories to take back into the cave with them. A significant pull of literature is to satisfy one's voyeuristic urges. A voyeur is "a prying observer who is usually seeking the sordid or the scandalous." People read to observe what otherwise wouldn't be so readily witnessed. There are conditions that must be met if the effort of looking, or reading, is to be worth the trouble.

There must be a sense of tension or electricity in the atmosphere of the hidden place. There must be enough sensuous detail to motivate the reader to feel in that place, in the present moment. The people being peeped in on, through their speech and gestures, must strike the reader as authentic and inspire both interest and a level of compassion. If these three elements are present, then the symbolic crouch outside the basement window, the figurative ear to the door, the invisible bugging of a room, the imaginary binoculars into the neighbour's apartment, make the experience of observing worthwhile.

Raymond Carver agrees with V.S. Pritchett's definition of the short story as "something glimpsed from the corner of the eye, in passing" (in Geddes 775). Carver has a gift for glimpsing worlds just enough off-kilter to warrant a sustained glance: "I like it when there is some feeling of threat or sense of menace in short stories ... it's good for the circulation" (775). It's this tension that keeps eyes riveted to the page or screen. Carver's writing is wall-to-wall eavesdropping into edgy moments in others' lives: lovers behind closed doors, sisters telling secrets, obsessed and jealous husbands. A reader is vitalized by seeing others in conflict. Frederick Busch believes good fiction is "the song inherent in the fighting through of people who share a room or house or bed or child or journey: they fear to perish of one another, or without each other" (in Metcalf 318). In order to hold or move the reader, a story must "try for its characters, or try its characters ... It makes us, with our secrets and lies, hurt ... it lets the darkness in" (in Metcalf 318).

It's the secrets uncovered that the voyeuristic reader is after. Mavis Gallant's protagonist Peter has a secret. He finds himself in a drunken co-worker's apartment. "She pressed her face and rubbed her cheek on his shoulder as if hoping the contact would leave a scar. He saw her back and her profile and his own face in the mirror over the fireplace. He thought, This is how disasters happen" ("Ice Wagon" in Grady 284). This woman "is the only secret Peter has from his wife" (288). The voyeuristic reader feels fortunate to have been entrusted with this knowledge.

Alice Munro pulls taut the suspense cord in *Lives of Girls and Women* by playing what's known against what's hidden: "the 'deep caves [are] paved with kitchen linoleum'; the touchable leads to the mysterious"

(Martin 60). Munro takes us to a familiar scene—ladies talking in the dining room, a male suitor drinking whisky and water, and a young girl Del asking for a sip. Against this very ordinary backdrop mounts a not so ordinary tension, as Del performs like a seal, hoping to win a taste of the forbidden.

> I went down on my knees ... barking my wonderful braying bark ... Mr. Chamberlain gradually lowered his glass and brought it close to my lips, withdrawing it, however, every time I stopped barking ... Mr. Chamberlain at last allowed my lips to touch the rim of the glass which he held in one hand. Then with the other hand he did something nobody could see. (in Geddes 525)

The reader is all eyes, anticipating that next wave of shock, the blast of adrenalin just around the next corner. The "touchable" intensifies tension in the film *Smooth Talk*, in which Treat Williams's character lounges outside against a screen door's frame while inside, Laura Dern's character quakes with ambivalence, caught between intense fear and excitement. Her familiar front hall is no longer safe. This electricity resulting from fearing and wanting and fearing the wanting is captured in the short story "Where Are You Going, Where Have You Been?"

> Connie stood barefoot on the linoleum floor, staring at him.
> "What do you want?" she whispered.
> "I want you," he said.
> "What?"
> "Seen you that night and thought, that's the one, yes sir. I never needed to look any more."
> "But my father's coming back. He's coming to get me. I had to wash my hair first—" She spoke in a dry, rapid voice, hardly raising it for him to hear.
> "No, your daddy is not coming and yes, you had to wash your hair and you washed it for me. It's nice and shining and all for me. I thank you sweetheart." (Oates, in Griffith 508)

A reader becomes breathless with fear.

In order to "go fearwards," Barbara Turner-Vesselago urges students in her writing classes to give all the sensuous details, the "moment by moment" details. These are what colour the images in the mind's eye and put the beads of perspiration on the brow, the fears in the heart. These are what cause the unbearable and strangely desirable shortness of breath for the reader. Besner talks about these sensuous details when naming Mavis Gallant's "talent for evoking a tangible cultural surround through meticulous attention to detail ... the more concrete, the more evocative" (26). George Woodcock also praises Mavis Gallant's ability to find "the impeccable verbal texture and the marvellous painterly surface ... that derives from a close and highly visual sense of the interrelation-ship of sharply observed detail" (93). Gallant knows that the description needs to be specific, not ornate. The reader can easily picture Gallant's character Sheilah as she pretends to a life she cannot afford.

> [Sheilah] put candles on the card table where she and Peter ate their meal. The neckline of the dress was soiled with make-up ... Behind her, at the kitchen table, Sandra and Jennifer, in buttonless pajamas and bunny slippers, ate their supper of marmalade sandwiches and milk. When the children were asleep, the parents dined solemnly, ritually, Sheilah sitting straight as a queen. ("Ice Wagon" in Grady 270)

Gallant conjures this somewhat pathetic image of a very particular life by taking the reader into the flat with the characters and watching them when they don't know they're being watched. The details com-municate the essence. Somehow the strong writer must be able to select which details are necessary to create "in the reader a feeling of verisimilitude—a sense that both individual elements and the whole fiction is like truth" (Jason and Lefcowitz 220). Well-selected details don't "recreate literal reality" but rather "an impression of it" (220). Strong writers are discerning in terms of which details warrant mention and manage to avoid "descriptive clutter" (228). Mavis Gallant de-scribes the writer's task as the artist who creates the page for a colouring book. The shapes must be there, but the colouring in is the task of the reader ("Morningside").

> Emily went into the [hotel] bathroom and shut the door. Francine heard the water running and then it stopped.
> "Mom," Emily called through the door. "Come here." Her voice sounded strange, excited.
> Francine went into the bathroom. Emily stood there naked, a pink towel wrapped around her head, staring at the mirror. The steam from the shower had brought out a message.
> 'Goodbye Harold, Good Luck.' Written by somebody's finger or with a piece of soap. (Thomas 221)

Through concrete details the reader not only pictures the scene but colours in the subtext, knowing the mother is contemplating her own desire to scribble an exit line to her husband and leave the wedding band she'd previously made obvious behind on the night table.

Alice Munro is equally excited "by what you might call the surface of life" (in Gibson 241). It is often the observation of "how things are" (241) and the "peculiarities in the world around her" (Stouck 260) that make Munro's world so alive and memorable. "That world is authenticated by the small textures" (260).

A piece of writing that truly satisfies a reader's voyeuristic urge is one in which the reader can hardly bear to look yet feels compelled to look, that makes the ordinary somehow seem extraordinary.

If readers are to feel satisfaction from spying on what ordinarily is hidden, they must believe and care about the character's struggles. "What is a narrative but a character in trouble? If I can see that character in action ... my cave-fire urges are satisfied. I'm willing to read him .... I am drawn into what happens next" (Metcalf 315). Readers are demanding. "My criterion is simply whether I like the author's voice and whether I can love the characters" (Brayfield 18). Author Sandra Birdsell puts it well: "I really love the people I'm writing about. I grew up with these women. I know what makes them cry, what makes them laugh" (in Twigg 19). She reveals her understanding of character when a lover says "God, you're beautiful" and Mika, the infidel, replies, "Don't say that" (in Geddes 65). Good fiction finds the familiar in the characters and includes whatever will have a reader saying, yes, I recognize this person. Good fiction "lies to tell the truth" (Besner 118). One of the challenges for the writer is to create characters who don't unduly threaten the reader's willingness to suspend disbelief. "Absolute plausibility demands absolute artifice, not faith to actuality" (in Woodcock 92). Gallant admits: "Even if a thing happened, if it's completely eccentric, there's no point in writing about it. If it isn't plausible, it doesn't matter. It's no good saying I assure you it happened" (106).

Saying it's true certainly isn't the answer. "Show, don't tell," was Diane Schoemperlen's daily plea to her writing class. It's in response to the showing that the readers feel glad they have troubled themselves for the glimpse. In Carver's story "Neighbours," the reader gets a clear picture of Bill Miller, watching him nosing about his neighbours' apartment while they're away, doing more than feeding their cat and watering their plants. He drinks their Chivas Regal, takes food from their fridge, pockets their medication and cigarettes, tries on their clothes, tries out their bed (in Stone, Packer, and Hoopes 507). The reader can sniff his envy over his neighbour's lives, his wish to change places, his excitement over stepping into their world for a while. His wife gets closer to naming the thrill when she confesses to finding photos in the neighbours' apartment and then says, astonished by her own words: "Maybe they won't come back" (510).

Munro's *Lives* was removed from the reading list in an Ontario high school because its characters are so authentic. "Essentially all they're objecting to is the truth" (Munro 216). Audrey Thomas's work also has this docu-fiction feeling. It has been described as "fictional in form but so close to life that the reader feels implicated in an unconscionable violation of privacy, despite assurances provided by the text itself that all is, in fact, fiction" (Moss 354). Readers crave seeing the hidden.

Authentic characters grip and unnerve the reader, in part due to their "identifiable way of speaking" (Jason and Lefcowitz 187). The reader welcomes the glimpse into character revealed through dialogue. "Through dialogue, we come to know a character directly. Dialogue is closer to life than anything else in fiction" (Schoemperlen). It's through dialogue that the writer captures reader interest, by both concealing and revealing (Schoemperlen). A scene is worth glimpsing when two or more textured characters brush up against each other for some kind of friction or chemical reaction. When one of her students expressed concern that the writing was always about relationships, Schoemperlen answered, "What else is there?" As long as the characters are authentic and motivated, what goes on between them will pull readers in. Carver's dialogue, interpreted by Altman, reveals plenty.

"You want me to get out of here? You've got it ..."
"No more. No more. I'm not taking you back, no more."
"... How come you don't wear your wedding ring to work any more?" the husband asks.
"You're such a bullshit artist."
"You're the one chipping away at our mansion of love, baby. Not me ..." (*Short Cuts*)

In "The Painted Door," a reader sees tension, detail, and characterization come together in one compelling, electric tale. A neighbour comes to keep his friend John's wife company, in his absence, during a prairie storm. There is electricity in Steven's voice.

"Not tonight—you might as well make up your mind to it. Across the hills in a storm like this—it would be suicide to try."

... She was afraid now. Afraid of his face so different from John's—of his smile, of her own helplessness to rebuke it. Afraid of the storm, isolating her here alone with   him." (Ross, in Lecker and David 315–316)

John's wife is scared, on edge with fear and thrill. "But he always came," she persisted. "The wildest, coldest nights—even such a night as this. There was never a storm ... Never a storm like this one" (in Lecker and David 317).

Ross finds the sensuous details, the bits of business, the gestures, the spilling of words, to create plausible characters in an impossible, dangerous situation. The reader can't turn the pages fast enough. The fact that "there was never a night like this" hooks the reader, keeps the reader reading.

There is magic in the ordinary, particularly when it's something not ordinarily seen. It is human to be curious, to wonder what goes on on the other side of the closed door, behind the drawn curtain. Strong writers manage to incite interest in what physical and psychological action blows at the curtains, rattles the windows, shakes the door. In the process, the reader is shaken. It is the gifted writer who knows how to build tension, select the most evocative moment-by-moment details, and appropriately conceal and reveal authentic character. As the next long, dark, cold season approaches, readers will seek the words of Birdsell, Carver, Gallant, Oates, Munro, Ross, Thomas, and other great writers. They'll search for the thrill and comfort of meeting, hearing, observing others with frailties, fears, intensely held emotions. People are curious creatures after all. Those writers who make visible the hidden will continue to turn pages, heads, and hearts.

WORKS CITED

Besner, Neil K. *The Light of Imagination: Mavis Gallant's Fiction.* Vancouver: University of British Columbia Press, 1988.

Birdsell, Sandra. In Conversation. *Strong Voices: Conversations with 50 Canadian Authors.* Alan Twigg. Madeira Park: Harbour, 1990. 19.

———."Night Travellers." *The Art of Short Fiction: An International Anthology.* Ed. Gary Geddes. Toronto: HarperCollins, 1993. 62, 65.

Brayfield, Celia. "My 10 Best Books." *Woman's Journal.* April 1994:18.

Busch, Frederick. *The New Story Writers.* Ed. John Metcalf. Kingston: Quarry, 1992. 318.

Carver, Raymond. "Neighbours." *The Short Story: An Introduction.* Ed. Wilfred Stone, Nancy Huddleston Packer, and Robert Hoopes. New York: McGraw-Hill, 1983. 507–510.

———."On Writing." *The Art of Short Fiction: An International Anthology.* Ed. Gary Geddes. Toronto: HarperCollins, 1993. 773.

Gallant, Mavis. Interview. *Morningside.* With Peter Gzwoski. Toronto: CBC Radio, n.d.

———. "The Ice Wagon Going Down the Street." *The Penguin Book of Modern Canadian Short Stories.* Ed. Wayne Grady. Markham: Penguin, 1988. 270, 284, 288.

———. Interview. *Strong Voices: Conversations with 50 Canadian Authors.* Alan Twigg. Madeira Park: Harbour, 1990. 106.

Jason, Philip K., and Allan B. Lefcowitz. *Creative Writer's Handbook.* 2nd ed. Englewood Cliffs, NJ: Prentice Hall, 1994.

Martin, W.R. *Alice Munro: Paradox and Parallel.* Edmonton: University of Alberta, 1987.

Metcalf, John, ed. *The New Story Writers.* Kingston, Ont.: Quarry Press, 1992.

Moss, John. *A Reader's Guide to the Canadian Novel.* 2nd ed. Toronto: McClelland & Stewart, 1987.

Munro, Alice. Interview. *Eleven Canadian Novelists.* Interviewed by Graeme Gibson. Toronto: Anansi, 1973. 241, 259.

———. Interview. *Strong Voices: Conversations with 50 Canadian Authors.* Alan Twigg. Madeira Park: Harbour, 1990. 216–217, 218.

———. "Lives of Girls and Women." *The Art of Short Fiction: An International Anthology.* Ed. Gary Geddes. Toronto: HarperCollins, 1993. 525.

Oates, Joyce Carol. Biographical Preface. *The Short Story: An Introduction.* Ed. Wilfred Stone, Nancy Huddleston Packer, and Robert Hoopes. New York: McGraw-Hill, 1983. 510.

———. "Where Are You Going, Where Have You Been?" *Narrative Fiction: An Introduction and Anthology.* Ed. Kelley Griffith. Orlando: Harcourt Brace, 1994. 508.

Ricou, Laurence. *Vertical Man/Horizontal World: Man and Landscape in Canadian Prairie Fiction.* Vancouver: University of British Columbia, 1973.

Ross, Sinclair. "The Painted Door." *The New Canadian Anthology: Poetry and Short Fiction in English.* Ed. Robert Lecker and Jack David. Scarborough: Nelson, 1988. 306–307, 315–317.

Schoemperlen, Diane. *Writing the Short Story.* Lecture Notes. Kingston, Ont.: Kingston School of Writing, July 18–24, 1993.

———. Personal interview. July 24, 1993.

Short Cuts. Dir. Robert Altman. Based on the writing of Raymond Carver. Alliance, 1994.

Smooth Talk. Dir. Joyce Chopra. With Treat Williams and Laura Dern. Vestron Video, 1985.

Stouck, David. *Major Canadian Authors: A Critical Introduction.* Nebraska: University of Nebraska Press, 1984.

Thomas, Audrey. Interview. *Strong Voices: Conversations with 50 Canadian Authors.* Madeira Park: Harbour, 1990. 251.

Turner-Vesselago, Barbara. *Freefall: Writing Without a Parachute.* Lecture. Golden Lake, Ont.: June 16–22, 1995.

Woodcock, George. *The World of Canadian Writing: Critiques and Recollections.* Vancouver: Douglas and McIntyre, 1980.

"Voyeur." *Webster's Ninth New Collegiate Dictionary.* 1985 ed.

COMMONLY MISSPELLED WORDS

absence	accidentally	accommodate
accumulate	achievement	acknowledgment
acquaintance	acquire	address
aggravate	all right	a lot
already	altogether	analysis
apparently	appearance	appropriate
argument	attendance	awful
basically	beginning	believe
benefited	bureaucracy	business
calendar	candidate	capital (city)
changeable	coincidence	commitment
colleague	committed	committee
competitive	complement	compliment
conceivable	conscience	conscientious
conscious	courageous	criticism
curiosity		
dealt	deceive	decision
definitely	dependable	dependent
description	desperate	desert (place)
dessert (food)	devastating	develop
disappear	disappoint	disastrous
dissatisfied		
eerie	eighth	eligible
embarrass	eminence	emphasize
enthralled	entrepreneur	environment
especially	exaggerate	excellent
exercise	existence	eyeing
facsimile	familiar	fascinate
February	foreign	forfeit
forty	fourth	

gauge
grammar

guarantee

government

height

herald

illiterate

incidentally

irrelevant

knowledgeable

leisure

licence (n) se (v)

loneliness

maintenance
monstrous

mischievous

misspell

necessary

noticeable

occasion

occurred/occurrence

paid
pastime
playwright
preference
principal (leader)
proceed
pursue

parallel
perseverance
practically
preferred
principle (idea)
professor

particularly
persistent
practice (n) se (v)
prejudice
privilege
prosperous

receive
referred
reminiscence
resemblance

recommend
relevant
renowned
rhythm

reference
relieve
repetition
roommate

sacrilegious
seize
similar
sponsor
strength
suing

schedule
separate
sincerely
stationary (still)
subtly
suppressed

scissors
siege
solely
stationery (paper)
succeed
surprise

temperamental
truly

theatre

tragedy

unmanageable	unnecessarily	usage
usually		

vacillate	vacuum	vengeance
villain		

weather (temperature)	Wednesday	weird
whether (or not)	wholly	wield
woman (singular)	women (plural)	wondrous

yield

NOT A WORD

alot	alright	anyways
anywheres		
could of		
everywheres		
hisself		
irregardless		
nowheres		
somewheres		
theirself, theirselves	themself	thusly
would of		

PERSONAL SPELLER

In the space below, keep track of the words that you have had to look up or have made mistakes with in the past. Instead of consulting the dictionary to check problem words, you can save time by consulting your list of personally troublesome words.

VOCABULARY LIST

In the space below, note down any new words you have encountered in your listening or reading. Include a sentence with the word properly used in it, and write a brief and easily understood definition of the word.

IRREGULAR VERBS

Infinitive	Past Tense	Past Participle
I like to begin early each day.	I began late yesterday	The phone has begun to ring.
arise	arose	arisen
awake	awoke	awaked
awaken	awakened	awakened
be	was, were	been
bear (to carry)	bore	borne
bear (to give birth)	bore	born
beat	beat	beaten, beat
become	became	become
begin	began	begun
bend	bent	bent
bite	bit	bitten, bit
blow	blew	blown
break	broke	broken
bring	brought	brought
build	built	built
burst	burst	burst
buy	bought	bought
catch	caught	caught
choose	chose	chosen
cling	clung	clung
come	came	come
cost	cost	cost
deal	dealt	dealt
dig	dug	dug
dive	dived, dove	dived
do	did	done
drag	dragged	dragged
draw	drew	drawn
dream	dreamed, dreamt	dreamed, dreamt
drink	drank	drunk
drive	drove	driven
drown	drowned	drowned
eat	ate	eaten
fall	fell	fallen

Infinitive	Past Tense	Past Participle
feel	felt	felt
fight	fought	fought
find	found	found
fit	fit, fitted	fit, fitted
fly	flew	flown
forbid	forbade, forbad	forbidden
forget	forgot	forgotten, forgot
freeze	froze	frozen
get	got	gotten, got
give	gave	given
go	went	gone
grow	grew	grown
hang (to suspend)	hung	hung
hang (to kill)	hanged	hanged
have	had	had
hear	heard	heard
hide	hid	hidden
hit	hit	hit
hurt	hurt	hurt
keep	kept	kept
know	knew	known
lay (to put)	laid	laid
lead	led	led
lend	lent	lent
let	let	let
lie (to recline)	lay	lain
light	lighted, lit	lighted, lit
lose	lost	lost
make	made	made
pay	paid	paid
prove	proved	proved, proven
put	put	put
read	read	read
ride	rode	ridden
ring	rang	rung
rise	rose	risen
run	ran	run
say	said	said
see	saw	seen

Infinitive	Past Tense	Past Participle
send	sent	sent
set (to place)	set	set
shake	shook	shaken
shine	shone, shined	shone, shined
shoot	shot	shot
shrink	shrank	shrunk, shrunken
shut	shut	shut
sing	sang	sung
sink	sank	sunk
sit	sat	sat
slay	slew	slain
sleep	slept	slept
speak	spoke	spoken
spin	spun	spun
split	split	split
spread	spread	spread
spring	sprang	sprung
stand	stood	stood
steal	stole	stolen
sting	stung	stung
strike	struck	struck, stricken
swear	swore	sworn
swim	swam	swum
swing	swung	swung
take	took	taken
teach	taught	taught
tear	tore	torn
throw	threw	thrown
wake	waked, woke	woken, waked
wear	wore	worn
win	won	won
wring	wrung	wrung
write	wrote	written

YOUR RULES OF THUMB

In the space below, name the organizational, punctuation, or mechanical problems you encounter most frequently in your writing. Note how to avoid the difficulty. Use any examples or document any words of wisdom that will make it easier for you to prevent or solve the problem in the future.

ONE DAY, SOME DAY

The discipline of the writer is to learn to be still and listen to what his subject has to tell him.

Rachel Carson (in Winokur 5)

In the space below, keep track of any interesting facts, good quotes, unusual thoughts, points of interest, dreams, doodles, noteworthy happenings, spontaneous ramblings, and other inspirational journal entries that could be the basis of ideas for future writing.

POSTSCRIPT

You do your best work when it brings you enjoyment and satisfaction. You write best when you know something about the topic and know what you want to stress. So when you can, write about a topic you've lived with and have considered over time. When you *have* to write about a topic that seems boring or difficult, get to know it for a while until it makes sense to you, until you can find a fresh way of looking at it that holds interest for you. Start with what is clear to you, and with what you care about, and you will write well.

Don't quit too soon. Sometimes a few more changes, a little extra attention to fine points, a new paragraph written on a separate piece of paper, will transform an acceptable piece of writing into a piece of writing that truly pleases both you and your readers. Through the time you spend writing and rewriting, you will discover what you have in you to say and how best to say it. I hope the ideas and rules of thumb in this book will help you develop your ability as a writer.

Take pleasure in the writing, and your reader will take pleasure in the reading.

INDEX